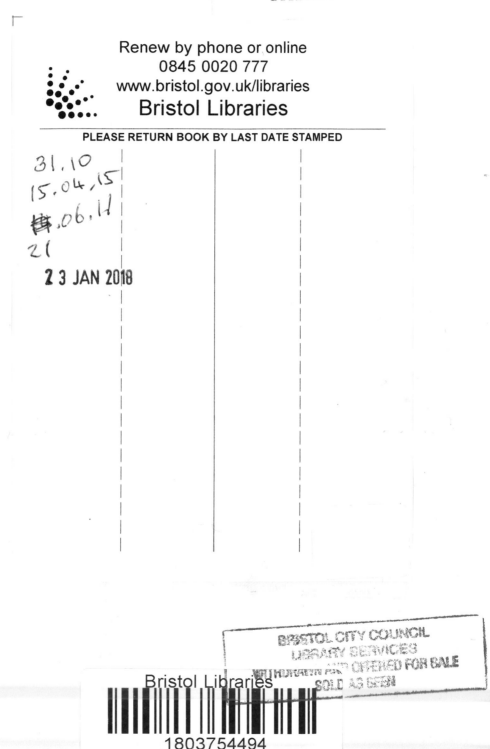

TALES FROM THE CONTROL TOWER

JOE BAMFORD

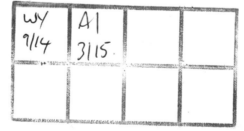

FONTHILL

Dedicated to Peter Turner, Ron Sadler and John Pulford of whom I have many happy memories. Also to the late Denis Todd, Chris Juhuboo and all those who worked in Air Traffic Control at RAF Manston.

FONTHILL MEDIA
www.fonthillmedia.com

First published by Fonthill Media 2012

Typeset in 11/13pt Bembo Std
Typesetting by Fonthill Media
Printed in the UK

ISBN 978-1-78155-041-0 (print)
ISBN 978-1-78155-157-8 (e-book)

Connect with us
 facebook.com/fonthillmedia   twitter.com/fonthillmedia

Contents

RAF Manston's original Gate Guardian, Spitfire TB752, with the control tower in the background, c. 1970. (*John Williams*)

Introduction

During the late 1960s, the structure of the Royal Air Force went through a series of radical changes that affected both the type of equipment that it operated and the manpower that was needed for its future commitments. Several new types of aircraft were introduced into service and on 30 April 1968, the command structure that had first been introduced in 1936 was replaced by Strike Command, an amalgamation of Bomber Command and Fighter Command. It was the first major move towards the RAF being controlled by a single command organisation.

Probably one of the other most significant changes at that time was the gradual retirement of those officers and senior NCOs who had served in the RAF during the Second World War. Their experience, knowledge and commitment had served the RAF well for over twenty-five years, but by the late 1960s they were surplus to requirements. After the war, large numbers of commissioned officers had been reduced to the ranks, while many of those who were fortunate enough to keep their commissions were duly demoted by two or three ranks. Subsequently, by the late 1960s there was a number of officers and senior NCOs who were of lower rank than they had been in 1945.

As the veterans of the Second World War approached the compulsory retirement age of fifty-five, they were gradually being replaced by a new breed of younger, career-orientated officers. Although the graduates from Cranwell were generally better educated than their predecessors, most of them not only lacked the character of earlier generations, but quite often their common sense as well. Many of the new breed of officers were only interested in impressing their seniors and attempting to get on to the next rung of the promotion ladder as soon as possible.

A number of types of aircraft that had served the air force well through the 1950s and early '60s were also being phased out of operational service in the late 1960s. Several piston-engined transport aircraft such as the Handley Page Hastings and the Blackburn Beverley were approaching their 'twilight' years and were being replaced by the Hawker Siddley Andover and the American-built C 130 Hercules, both of which were powered by modern turbo-prop engines. The Vampire and the Javelin fighters were also in the process of being withdrawn as another American type, the F 4 Phantom, was about to enter into service.

It was only after the TSR 2 project had been abandoned by the labour government in April 1965 that the F 4 Phantom was chosen to join the RAF fleet. The decision to purchase American-built aircraft was a controversial one; it was suggested that the British Government had only bought them to repay American Government support during a financial crisis. The original order had been for fifty American-built F 111A aircraft, but that was cancelled by Harold Wilson's government in favour of the Phantoms.

However, not all the new types of aircraft entering service with the RAF were American; the Hawker Siddley Nimrod, the Hawker Siddley Harrier, and the Blackburn Buccaneer proved the capabilities of the British Aircraft Industry. There was also the English Electric Lightning, which although often referred to as a 'Fighter', was recognised by the experts as an 'Interceptor'. Whether or not it was a fighter or an interceptor, the Lightning was a very capable aircraft and an integral part of Britain's Air Defence capability.

The RAF celebrated its 50th anniversary on 1 April 1968, but the main celebrations did not take place until 14 June, when a Royal Review took place at RAF Abingdon. One officer, Flight Lieutenant Alan Pollock, a flight commander on 1 Squadron, was so disgruntled at the anniversary not being held on the day that he made his own protest to Harold Wilson. On 5 April, after taking off from Tangmere in Sussex in Hawker Hunter XF442, Pollock flew over London and buzzed the Houses of Parliament three times before flying under Tower Bridge. As one might expect, he was charged and would have been court martialled had he not been invalided out of the RAF before it could take place. The decision to discharge him on medical grounds probably saved the government a lot of embarrassment and prevented ministers from losing face.

At Abingdon in June, thirty-one Jet Provosts took part in the opening fly past in a formation that represented the letters 'E II R'. That was followed by another fly past by a wide variety of aircraft that had been used by the RAF in its fifty years of existence.

1968 was also a very a special year because it was then that the film *The Battle of Britain* was made; it reminded everyone about the sacrifice of the 'few'. RAF Manston had a key role in the film even before it was made because all the German aircraft that featured in it landed there to be inspected by the Board of Trade. Many of the realistic air combat scenes were filmed over the south coast of England; the aircraft that took part in the film flew from airfields like Hawkinge near Folkestone, which had actually played an active role back in 1940. The film closely followed events that had taken place during the battle and it was a great tribute to both the airmen of the Royal Air Force and the Luftwaffe.

The manned strength of the RAF on 2 July 1968 was 120,337 regular servicemen, over four times the strength of today's air force. The RAF was in fact larger in 1968 that it had been on the outbreak of war, when its strength had amounted to just 101,199 servicemen. Technology and changing political climates have often been used as excuses for reductions in the numbers of personnel, but in 1969 it might have been argued that it was a change of role in the RAF that gave credence to such cuts.

Twenty-nine years after the Battle of Britain, the primary role of the RAF was to carry out a retaliatory nuclear air attack in the event of nuclear war. This role was handed over to the Royal Navy and its newly commissioned fleet of Polaris submarines. Each submarine was capable of carrying sixteen 31-foot-long Polaris A3 missiles. That huge change in defence planning was arranged to take place on 30 June 1969, to coincide with the commissioning of the Royal Navy's third nuclear submarine, HMS *Renown*, which joined HMS *Resolution* and HMS *Repulse* into service.

After the handover, the RAF's 'V' bomber force was effectively made redundant, but it was assigned to operate in a new tactical low-level role. For the RAF it was the end of an era. The Vulcan's distinctive 'anti-flash' white paint was gradually replaced by a new grey-green camouflage scheme, and like the Handley Page Victor, its role was converted to Electronic Counter Measures (ECM) and that of an airborne tanker. Both types continued to serve well for many more years; Britain still had a 'V' bomber force in all but name.

Tales From The Control Tower is my own personal account of life in the RAF, during what I consider to be one of the most interesting periods of its post-war history. The story covers the period from July 1968 to May 1971, and follows events and incidents that were never made public. It tells of my own experiences during basic training at Swinderby, and then of my posting to the former 'V' Bomber Station at Gaydon in Warwickshire, then of my time at RAF Shawbury, where I trained as an Assistant Air Traffic Controller, and finally my experiences at RAF Manston in Kent, which was my first operational posting.

This is a true account of life in the RAF during the late 1960s and early '70s, warts and all! Where I have thought it necessary, I have changed names to protect the identities of both the innocent and the guilty, but in most cases I have used real names, and have fond memories of my old colleagues!

CHAPTER 1

Joining Up

Like many young boys in the 1960s, I left school at the age of 15 without any formal educational qualifications, but nevertheless, I had no trouble in getting a job. It was July 1966 and my first employment was at Ward & Goldstones on Frederick Road in Salford, where my father worked in the spark-testing department as a supervisor. I started my working life as an electrical engineering apprentice, but it soon became clear that the job was not for me, and after only a few months I decided to leave.

I soon got another job working for Radio Rentals on cathode ray tubes at a factory in Salford where I had the best job of all – watching television all day, even if it was only the BBC test card. When a horse racing meeting was being televised and the boss was not around, I would plug in the external aerial and everyone would stop work and crowd around the test set, normally to see their horses lose! It was all good fun, but although I was promised a job as a trainee TV engineer, I decided to move on.

From the very beginning, I found the humdrum of factory or shop work boring; I wanted to break away from the tedious routine and do something different. Most of my evenings and weekends were spent on the terraces at Manchester Airport aircraft spotting. Aircraft and aviation were undoubtedly the most important things in my life. The sound of the Rolls-Royce Tyne that powered the Vickers Vanguard was music to my ears, and the smell of kerosene that hung in the air at the airport always gave me a buzz!

On 1 January 1966, I flew for the first time on board the BEA Vanguard G-APEA from Manchester to London. I was fortunate that in my youth I gained a considerable amount of flying experience, mostly on airliners like the Vicker's Vanguard and Viscount. The return fare was £6-14 shillings; as

I was still at school it fell to my parents to fund my travels, but I helped out by doing various small jobs whenever I could. From the first moment that I boarded the aircraft I was hooked, and Queens Building at Heathrow almost became my second home.

In October 1967, I ventured further afield and flew from London to Paris on board an Air France Boeing 707, returning the same evening to Heathrow on an Air France Caravelle. I had arranged to stay overnight in Paris but after seeing the sights and going up to the third stage of the Eiffel Tower I decided to go home early and flew back to Manchester that evening.

At Manchester Airport a former RAF pilot, Bruce Martin, often took me and other enthusiasts up in his Auster Autocar (G-AOBV) at the end of the day as a reward for drumming up custom for his pleasure flights or washing the aircraft down. Bruce owned a company called Air Views whose main business was aerial photography. At weekends he competed for passengers with Northern Executive Aviation, which operated a modern Piper Cherokee (G-ARVS) that was more modern and often more popular

An Invicta International Vanguard on the apron at RAF Manston, in front of the airline's operations building. This former Air Canada (CF-TKF) aircraft was one of seven operated by Invicta between 1971 and September 1976, when this particular aircraft was sold to a French company. The author had his very first flight in this type of aircraft with BEA on 1 January 1966.

with the public. However, Bruce was more likely to give his passengers a more realistic experience of flying than could ever be achieved in the Cherokee.

One evening while I was at Manchester Airport I was invited to a talk that was being given by two members of the newly formed RAF Red Arrows aerobatic team. They told those of us that were present about the history of the team and why they personally had decided to join the RAF, and then later apply to join the Red Arrows. Most of us came away from the talk feeling very excited; meeting such interesting people greatly influenced my direction in life. So much so that from that moment onwards, if I had not already made my mind up to join the RAF, I decided that it was where my future lay.

I was just 16 years old when I first applied to join the RAF, and on 3 April 1967 I was invited to attend the Youth Selection Centre at RAF Stafford. I had applied to become a craft apprentice, and along with another thirty or so hopeful young men, I spent two days at Stafford undergoing medical examinations and an aptitude test. Out of all the applicants in my group, only two made the grade and unfortunately I was not one of them. However, the RAF did not reject me totally, and I was told to apply again when I became eligible for regular service at the age of seventeen.

However, after being turned down by the RAF I felt a little hurt; I decided that the air force's loss would be the army's gain! Some of my family had served in the army with distinction during the First World War; both my grandfather, Enoch Holland, and his brother Joe had served with the 16th Battalion of the Lancashire Fusiliers (2nd Salford Pals). In 1917 both brothers were awarded the Military Medal and were mentioned in Dispatches. During my early childhood I was inspired by my grandmother who proudly displayed grandfather's medals and told me stories about his heroic deeds in the trenches.

Some time later I learned that my late Uncle Frank, who had served with the 8th Battalion of the Lancashire Fusiliers in India, had been killed at the infamous battle at Kohima in April 1944. My mother's cousin, Fusilier Edward Ryan had also served in the Lancashire Fusiliers and he had been killed near Rangoon in Burma in 1943. Hearing stories about them increased my interest in the army even more, and I fancied following in the footsteps of my relatives, but preferably without being maimed or killed.

Because I was always more far more interested in aviation than guns, soldiering or other aspects of the military, I thought I would apply to join the Army Air Corps instead.

In early 1968 I arranged an interview at the Careers Information Office in Fountain Street, Manchester, to process my application to join the army. While I was waiting to be called in, a flight sergeant from the RAF began talking to me and asked why I wanted to join the army? I told him about my previous application to join the RAF and how I had been rejected. I also said that despite my limited academic qualifications, the Army Air Corps offered the best opportunity for me to train as a pilot.

The flight sergeant smiled as he listened to me and he seemed to be mildly amused by what I was saying. He then told me that things were not always as they seemed and that before I could apply to join the Army Air Corps I would have to train as a regular soldier and join a regiment. Another stumbling block was that officers and senior NCOs normally had to serve for at least four years before they could volunteer to join the Army Air Corps, and even then there was no guarantee that a soldier would be accepted.

He went on to explain that those who were lucky enough to be selected for aircrew training in the army were sent to the Aircrew Selection Centre at Biggin Hill where they went through exactly the same test and selection procedures as prospective RAF aircrew. Finally, after a four year tour in the Army Air Corps, aircrew were often returned to their regiments to resume their normal duties! Suddenly the army did not seem quite such an attractive proposition after all, and although half-heartedly I still went through with the interview, I changed my mind again and decided to join the RAF!

The flight sergeant was glad to have me back and he gave me a booklet called 'Man On The Ground' which described life in the RAF in all its glory and what an airman could expect from the service. The section entitled 'Your Life' said that it was the men on the ground that kept the aircraft in the air and it made it sound very exciting. The booklet highlighted the new aircraft that were entering service with the RAF such as the Belfast and the VC10, the latter being able to fly to Singapore in 18 hours in two stages, with one stop in Cyprus and another on the remote island of Gan in the Indian Ocean.

It is interesting to note that the aircraft that later became known as the Nimrod was described in the booklet as the 'Comet HS 801'. Over forty years later, both the VC10 and the Nimrod were still in RAF service. In fact in 2007, another version of the Nimrod, the Mk MRA4 (a victim of George Osbourne's Defence Review in 2011, and destroyed in a fit of economic madness) was being built at Woodford and I was privileged to witness the final stage of the assembly. Sadly, the Belfast became something of a white elephant and the RAF sold them off in September 1976.

The person who influenced me most prior to joining the RAF was Senior Aircraftsman Bob Bailey, who I had met on the terraces at Manchester Airport. Bob had served in the Far East and had only recently returned from Gan, proudly wearing the ribbon of the General Service Medal on his chest. Being several years older than me and much more experienced, Bob had the great ability to spin a yarn; with his stories of the Far East he made life in the RAF sound like one huge adventure. Bob was an assistant air traffic controller and he convinced me that air traffic control was the trade to be in, and so the List 2 Trade, Trade Group 9, Assistant Air Traffic Controller was what I opted for.

At Fountain Street in Manchester, I passed the RAF's aptitude test with flying colours and I was advised by the staff at the Careers Information Office to train in the List 1 Trade as an Aircraft Fitter Propulsion (Engine Fitter). Even up to the point of attestation on 1 July, the flight sergeant there pleaded with me to change my mind and train in a technical trade, but I decided to stay with air traffic. Having gone through attestation and received the 'King's Shilling', everything happened very quickly. Within three days I became a fully paid up member of the Royal Air Force.

CHAPTER 2

RAF Swinderby

On Thursday 4 July 1968 I travelled from my home in Pendlebury, Manchester, to begin my basic training at RAF Swinderby in Lincolnshire. I travelled to the railway station in Manchester on my own in a taxi, so that the final farewells with my parents could be said at home and any emotional outbursts would be in private! In the course of the next six years that I served in the RAF, the experience of leaving friends and family behind never got any easier, and in fact as time went on it only got harder!

As I waited at Manchester Piccadilly for my train to Sheffield, I had plenty of time to reflect on recent events and I was full nervous anticipation about what lay ahead. A smartly dressed man caught my attention because he was carrying what I identified as an RAF holdall. We made the usual small talk about the weather and the train being late and then we went our separate ways, pacing up and down the platform waiting for it to arrive.

When I eventually arrived at Victoria Road Station in Sheffield, I discovered that not only did I have to change trains, but stations as well and walk across town to Sheffield Midland Station, which was some distance away. Having got there I discovered that there was to be another long wait for the connection to Retford, where I was to board a London-bound train for the third and final part of my journey to Newark. Having arrived later than expected at Retford, I found that the London train was just pulling into the platform; at a passing glance I could see that every carriage was packed and there was to be standing room only.

It was at this about this point that I met up again with the chap who I had briefly spoken to while we had been waiting on the platform at Piccadilly Station. Apart from the fact that he was carrying a large blue canvas bag that

I had identified as an RAF holdall, I now observed that he had the posture and haircut to suggest that he was already a serviceman. We were pushed together in the tightly packed corridor by the door, and as we got chatting, he confirmed that he had already served in the RAF for five years and that he was also on his way to Swinderby to join up again. Having only recently been discharged from the service he had found himself unable to settle down in 'civvy street' and so he had decided his only option was to go back into the RAF.

My new friend's name was John; he came from Blackpool and seemed confident and knowledgeable about what lay ahead of us at Swinderby. I told him about some of the horror stories that I had heard concerning discipline at RAF training stations like Padgate and Bridgnorth. I had read quite a few stories about life in the RAF and more than a few of them concerned the sadistic actions of officers and senior NCOs. One account was of a senior officer who always wore white cotton gloves during barrack room inspections; he ran his fingers across cupboards and floors looking for the slightest trace of dust. It was also claimed that he was so keen to catch airmen out, that he even ran his fingers under the rim of the toilet, just to discover whether it had been cleaned properly.

In the 1950s, offenders were treated harshly. 'Jankers', as it was referred to in the service, involved the offending airman reporting to the guard room twice a day in best blue uniform with a full pack on his back that carried all his kit. The reporting times were normally first thing in the morning and last thing at night, when he and his kit were closely inspected by the orderly officer. Another favourite punishment involved airmen being ordered to 'paint coal black'; individual pieces were taken out of a coal scuttle, painted, then put into a bucket that was full of mucky coal dust. When the airman had finished he had to start all over again until the duty corporal or sergeant decided he had done enough. A similar sadistic punishment involved airmen being ordered to paint the white lines on the parade ground – with a toothbrush!

Despite my colleague's reassurances that the RAF had changed since those dark distant days, his jocular attempts to put me at ease as we neared our destination failed miserably. I felt increasingly anxious about what I would experience and I began to have second thoughts about the commitment I had made just a few days before in Manchester. As we got off the train and walked through the concourse of Newark Station, further attempts by my new companion to raise my spirits failed miserably and my mood was darkening by the minute!

As I looked around, I observed that the station was full of young men, all looking equally anxious and carrying a variety of bags and suitcases, which, like mine, probably contained their most treasured possessions. A blue Bedford bus awaited our arrival and a corporal stepped down and began to shout for recruits to pay attention. It was noticeable that he was dressed in an immaculate best blue uniform, topped off with a 'slashed' peak cap; he seemed to be setting a standard that was almost impossible for us new recruits to attain.

The first thing that he told us was that his name was Corporal Fagg, and with the two outstretched fingers of his right hand he pointed to the two stripes on the left arm of his tunic. He informed us that he was a Junior Non-Commissioned Officer, and we should address him as 'Corporal'. Anyone who called him 'Sir' would be in trouble and if they persisted in doing so they would be put on a charge!

We were informed that only commissioned officers and warrant officers were to be addressed as 'Sir' and if anyone called them 'Corporal', then they really would be in trouble! There was suppressed laughter at this remark and then he asked us if there were any questions? There were none, probably because after the corporal's introduction everyone was frightened of making a fool of themselves. Not surprisingly, it suddenly went very quiet!

Corporal Fagg then called out our names in alphabetical order and as we answered he ticked them off his list that was attached to a clipboard. As we stepped forward, we showed him our papers before boarding the bus, but it was a very slow process. Some recruits had forgotten the 'arrival letters' we had been given at the Careers Information Office, and it took quite a while for the corporal to sort out everybody's paperwork.

Not all the recruits that Corporal Fagg was expecting turned up and so we had to wait for another train to arrive, but when they did not appear on that one either, he seemed rather agitated. From what bits of information we could gather, it seemed that at least two recruits had changed their minds and decided prematurely that the RAF was not for them. Eventually, about three-quarters-of-an-hour after our arrival, Corporal Fagg boarded the bus and we were finally on our way to RAF Swinderby to accept our fate as determined by the training syllabus of Number 7 School of Recruit Training.

Number 7 School of Recruit Training, where all adult recruits underwent initial training, had originally been formed in October 1945 at Bridgnorth in Shropshire. Its facilities had been transferred to Swinderby in June 1964 and the RAF claimed that it was the largest recruit training organisation in the UK for the armed forces. We were to spend six weeks at RAF Swinderby, and in that time we would receive a thorough introduction to the customs, traditions and procedures of service life.

The course included the basic elements of service life such as discipline, drill, arms drill and the care and maintenance of a service rifle. Also the basic principles of passive defence that we could use in nuclear war, an event that everyone hoped would never happen. I was a little sceptical, if not puzzled, to know how one could be passive in the event of a nuclear war but I was sure that would all be explained in due course!

The first building we were taken to after our arrival was the Airmens' Mess for a late tea that consisted of sausages, beans, chips and mashed potato and more beans. The tea itself had to be poured out from a large stainless steel electric urn, and it tasted particularly strong and foul. At this point I did not know why and I had never heard of bromide or its potentially debilitating effects! The meal was a fairly casual affair but everyone was still quite nervous, making polite conversation as we got to know one another. It all felt very unreal, the calm before the storm that would be unleashed at any moment, and on that point I was not wrong!

After we had eaten we were told to wait outside the mess and eventually, when everybody had finished, we were ordered to form up into ranks of three for our first taste of RAF discipline and drill. We were lined up with the tallest man on the left, from whom we took our dressing before being marched off down the road. I use the term 'marched' in the loosest possible sense because the whole procession was something of a shambles with arms and legs moving in all directions. Hardly anyone was in step and some recruits looked as though they were just taking a casual evening stroll in the park, but the reality of our situation soon hit us when we were called to a halt at our destination, the camp barbers.

Everyone expressed some surprise when Corporal Fagg informed us that nobody was exempt from having their haircut, no matter how short it was already. Possibly to avoid an encounter with the barber, some recruits had already had their hair cut short, while others were still proudly sporting their long precious locks. In those distant days of hippies and free love, long hair was the norm and short hair nearly always gave away the fact that the bearer was either a policeman or in the forces. Being taken to the barber might have been the first surprise, but the second one came when we were told that we also had to pay for the privilege.

A small number of recruits moaned pitifully and claimed that they had no money but their excuses were dismissed immediately when Corporal

Fagg announced that those who could not pay would be given a loan. The money would then be deducted from our first pay parade the following week. Amazingly, those who had made the most fuss suddenly went quiet and everyone had their hair cut and paid up without further comment. On the question of future hair cuts, Corporal Fagg informed us that it was an offence in the RAF for an airman not to have about his person enough money for the price of a haircut. We were warned that should anyone try that excuse again they could be charged, not for the cost of the haircut, but on the RAF Form 252 Disciplinary Form.

After parading outside the barber's shop, we were split up into flights and marched the short distance along the road to the Bedding Stores, where we were issued with three blankets (two dark, one white), two sheets, a single pillowcase and a colourful bed cover. I was assigned to Number 2 Flight under the guidance of Corporal Good and Sergeant Tewnion. Carrying our bedding in our outspread arms we marched and stumbled the short distance to our accommodation blocks where we were assigned to our rooms – 'home' for the next month and a half. The room we were allocated was on the first floor of what was essentially a typical RAF 'H' block, a two-storey building made of modern red brick.

Down each side of our room were ten equally spaced metal-framed beds; rather remarkably we were allowed to select the one that we wanted. Each bed had a mattress and a pillow on it, most of them stained and marked to suggest that they were well worn. Immediately on the right beside each bed was a small wooden locker for one's toiletries, personal possessions and small kit. Next to that was a tall locker that acted as a wardrobe where we hung our civilian clothes, our uniforms and some of our personal possessions.

The floor consisted of dark brown lino that looked old and worn and although there were bright shiny patches under the beds where it had been polished, most of it was dirty and badly scuffed. Corporal Fagg now informed us that the immediate area around each of our beds was our own personal responsibility and it had to be swept and polished every morning for inspection. For those of us who had had our own rooms at home, the bed space was minute and the total lack of privacy came as something of a shock!

Having already announced that he was our instructor and introduced us to our humble accommodation, Corporal Fagg then treated us to a demonstration of how to make a 'bed pack'. Those among us who thought that sheets and blankets were for sleeping in were in for a surprise; our corporal gathered us around in a large group and began to demonstrate how we should fold the bedding into what he described as a nice neat sandwich! This involved folding up the blankets and sheets in a very precise and neat manner to form an oblong shaped bundle of bedding presented in the prescribed order. At the centre of the pack was the white blanket with a sheet placed on either side of it and the dark blankets formed the bottom and top layers. The green and yellow bed cover was then wrapped around the bundle of sheets and blankets to form the perfect oblong shape, just like a sandwich.

After his demonstration, Corporal Fagg told us to get on with it, saying that when he returned he expected to see our bed packs made up just as he had shown us. However, when he came back half-an-hour or so later he was less than happy with what he found; in most cases our efforts to follow his instructions to produce a perfectly symmetrical bed pack had gone, literally, pear-shaped! A few former servicemen were among the only ones who succeeded and among them was John, the chap I had met on the journey from Manchester to Sheffield. He tried to guide me through the process but I could not get the hang of it; at the end of a long day I was feeling very tired and fed up!

Corporal Fagg did not give up on us easily and he threatened to keep us up all night if necessary, but after a while he became very frustrated and said he was going to leave and would return early the next morning. He ordered us to get to bed and muttered curses under his breath as he marched off down the corridor, turning off lights and slamming doors along the way. True to his word, at 6 a.m. the following morning, just after Reveille had sounded over the tannoy, he appeared standing in the doorway and so began the process all over again.

Those airmen who were suddenly woken up from sweet dreams were soon experiencing a living nightmare as our corporal chased us around to make sure that we were up, getting dressed and ready for parade. Leading men had been assigned to each room and fortunately for me, my friend John was chosen as one of them and he helped me sort myself out. After we had completed our ablutions we had to sweep our bed space and polish and bumper the floor until it shone like glass. A bumper is big square lump of iron with a cloth like a large duster on the end of it attached to a broom handle. Huge dollops of Mansion House polish were applied to the floor by recruits down on their hands and knees with bits of blanket tucked under their legs to avoid scratching the floor. The bumper was then repeatedly pushed backwards and forward to polish the floor until you could almost see your reflection.

At some point during the proceedings we had to go the airmen's mess for breakfast and shove whatever was served up into our mouths and down our throats as quickly as possible. Most of us were not hungry but we had been warned not to miss breakfast because if we fell ill or sick due to not eating, it was a chargeable offence. Subsequently, breakfast for most us was just a piece of buttered toast washed down with ill-tasting tea or coffee.

When breakfast was over we had to run back to the block and make or finish making up our bed packs and prepare our lockers for inspection, before quickly getting dressed and preparing for early morning parade at 7.30 a.m. During the inspection and parade nearly every other recruit was picked up for petty infringements; offenders had their names taken and were put on report. Fortunately I was one of the lucky ones who escaped close scrutiny, and by time Corporal Fagg got to my end of the line I think his note book must have been full!

After the parade we were marched off to the clothing store where we were issued with the standard RAF holdall to help us carry our uniform and kit. Then, in no particular order, came underwear, pyjamas, PT vest, shorts, plimsoles, shoes, boots, shirts, separate collars and studs, sweaters, ties, webbing belt and hats. We were not issued berets at this stage of training, but only the stupid looking flat-peaked hats that everyone hated. Even after completing basic training, only those airmen who were in a technical trade were officially issued with berets and the rest of us had to beg, steal or borrow them!

Much of our equipment had to be squeezed into the holdalls; the large blue canvas bag was one of the most important pieces of kit that we were ever issued with. However, it did not, as its name suggests, 'hold all', and much of our equipment had to be carried in our arms. Much of to the disgust of Corporal Fagg, a large number of items were dropped on the ground as we paraded again outside; the offenders were cajoled and made to pick them up.

Having collected our bits and pieces of uniform and secured them back in the lockers in our rooms, we were marched down to the photographic section where we had our photographs taken for our identity card, known in the RAF as Form 1250. As we had not been issued with our proper uniforms, we had to wear a 'bib' with a false collar and tie, to make it look as though we were properly attired. The process seemed quite fraudulent and although we were told to smile, not surprisingly, very few did.

The leather uppers of our boots, that we had to start wearing immediately for up to 8 hours a day, were very hard and we had to rub them with lots of dubbing and polish to soften them. Inevitably, within a few days most of us got huge blisters and it was not until the skin on our tender young feet hardened that the boots began to feel comfortable. The service issue shoes (Bata) were the typical black standard type with large toe caps that also had to be highly polished. We only wore the shoes in the evening for walking out; after wearing heavy boots all day, they felt like carpet slippers.

The standard issue RAF shirts were the collarless 'Granddad' type, and very few of us had ever worn such garments before. The separate collars were starched and as stiff as cardboard so it took a real effort to thread the stud through at the back of the neck. There was a second stud through the front of the collar that was equally hard to connect and those of us with nimble fingers soon developed blisters on them to match those on our feet!

At about the same time we were measured up for our RAF uniforms, but in such a casual fashion that it seemed as though the tailors, if that is what they were, failed to take into account the fact that we might be wearing the same one for many years to come. Rough measurements of leg and chest were taken but nobody seemed too bothered about accuracy and a few inches here and there appeared not to matter. It would be a week before any of us would actually wear a full uniform and even longer for those airmen whose trousers and tunics had to be sent back for alterations.

This was probably the most depressing part of our basic training because we had to parade and drill while still wearing elements of our civilian clothing, such as our jackets and trousers. There were various styles and colours on display and they clearly did not fit in with the service hats and hobnail boots.

It is often said that if you do not look the part, you do not feel the part, and that was certainly the case with most of us during the first the first week of training at Swinderby! To this day it still reminds me of a scene from the film 'Dad's Army', in which Captain Mannering's platoon of the Home Guard get their uniforms in dribs and drabs as they marched along the road. That great comedy programme was first shown on BBC Television the 9 July 1968, just five days after I arrived at Swinderby, and it proved to me that the humour based on the bad organisation of the forces was still alive and well!

Now that we had our basic uniform and kit, it all had to be laid out each morning on the bottom of our beds for inspection, exactly as prescribed by the large poster on the wall of our room. Every item had to be put in the correct place as per the photograph, and failure to follow this exacting procedure meant that the recruit would be put on report. Shoes, webbing belt, button stick, spare shirts, pyjamas, P.T. kit and bed pack had to be put on display.

Anything less than perfect symmetry was not tolerated and although we normally checked each others' lay out, someone always fell foul of Corporal Fagg or our flight commander, Flight Lieutenant Woodward. Whenever he or another officer entered our room, the accompanying NCO would shout out, 'Officer in the room. Stand by your beds!' At that point, no matter what we were doing or our state of dress we had to snap to attention, stand facing towards the officer and await further instructions. On one or two occasions that lead to some embarrassing moments, especially when an airman was finishing off his ablutions in a state of undress. However, an order was an order and one had to stand to attention as best as one could, whatever little one was wearing!

During those first few weeks we were at the bottom of the pile as far as the RAF was concerned, and just to add insult to injury, when we were on parade and the recruits of the senior flight marched past us they would often shout abusive comments like, 'Look at the green sprogs! Is the ink on your 1250 dry yet?' and 'Get some in!' There were many others remarks that are not fit for print, but the junior and senior NCOs never interfered or disciplined anyone. Everyone accepted the abuse as part of the training ritual and the rite of passage!

Apart from the fact that we clearly stood out because we were not wearing full RAF uniform, we were also recognised by the colour of the plastic discs that we had to wear behind our cap badge. The colour of the badge corresponded with the stage of weekly training, and they were changed every Monday to either blue, green, yellow or white badges. During the sixth and final week of training, no disc was worn at all, but just the RAF badge. However, for the first week we displayed a red badge to indicate that we were just a bunch of 'sprogs' that were a danger to ourselves and anyone else we came into contact with! We were treated accordingly by the majority of junior NCOs and recruits from the senior flights.

Swinderby was typical of most RAF stations in that it was separated into two distinct areas or sites: a domestic site and an airfield site. On the domestic site there was the Navy, Army and Air Force Institute (NAAFI), airmen's mess, accommodation blocks, stores and administration offices. To get from our accommodation block and on to the airfield site we had to cross a busy road, and that could only be achieved by our corporal acting like a traffic cop and stopping the traffic. Most of the drill we did was carried out on the vast expanse of the airfield site, either in the open or in the hangars when it rained, but there was a parade ground on the domestic site that was occasionally used.

Most weekday mornings were taken up with drill lessons, and the afternoon's activities varied between a number of other subjects, continuing until 4.30 p.m.

At lunchtime on Saturdays we were normally stood down until Monday morning, except for the first weeks when Corporal Fagg informed us that we would have to attend Church parade the following day. Because we were not properly attired in uniform, he told us that our first Sunday Church parade would just be for training purposes, and our first proper Church parade would be held the following week. As we were a scruffy bunch of urchins without uniforms he said that we would be the last to enter the church and that we would have to stand at the back.

On the Sunday morning as we turned out for parade, we were reminded that it was not compulsory to go into the church and those who genuinely objected on religious grounds, or those who were not members of the Church of England were exempt. A few minutes later when Corporal Fagg suddenly gave the order, 'Roman Candles, take one step forward!' The blank expressions on everyone's faces proved that nobody knew what he was talking about. In sheer frustration he shouted out, 'For Christ sake, aren't any of you Rat Catchers?... Oh for God's sake ... are any of you bloody Catholics?' I later learned that this was Corporal Fagg's own version of a genuine command used on RAF parades, 'Fall out Roman Catholics and Jews', which was genuinely given on a Church parade before airmen entered church.

Eventually the penny dropped and a small number of airmen shuffled forward and were quickly led away to form another separate rank, before being quickly dismissed. The rest of us were warned again that although we had the right to object to attending the church service, if any of us did so they would have to answer to Flight Lieutenant Woodward. Unless an individual airman had genuine reasons based on religious grounds (as a small number had already registered), then he would probably be put on a charge.

With an air of authority in his voice, Corporal Good then shouted out loud, 'Does anyone object to attending Church parade?' Nobody said a word and we were led off inside the church like lambs to the slaughter. This was my first experience of the RAF's compulsory religion, but it would not be the last.

Within the first week we were subjected to medical examinations to assess our fitness levels and so that the RAF could decide what medical category to put us in. The highest medical grade for ground crew was A4 G1 Z1. The letter 'A' indicated an individual's suitability for aircrew, so subsequently only pilots and other aircrew categories ever reached A1. The letter 'G' indicated an airmen's ability to use firearms and to perform on the ground in a particular role such as Ground Defence. Finally the letter 'Z' indicated whether there were any restrictions on the regions or 'Zones' abroad to where an airman could be posted. For instance, for some airmen a posting to a country with a hot tropical climate could raise a number of health issues.

The medical examination was quite strict with fingers and probes being stuck into every orifice that one could imagine, and a few that a young, healthy seventeen-year-old did not know anything about! We were given injections for every disease known to man including TB, Cholera and Tetanus. It is often said that grown men collapse at the sight of a needle but at my medical it actually happened; a number of recruits fainted or were frightened and made a fuss about having a needle stuck into them. Rather typically, it turned out that they were the bullies and big mouths who up to that point had had a lot to say. Having lost face in front of our instructors and other recruits, most of them quietened down and began to fall into line.

One recruit was found to have flat feet and was discharged immediately on medical grounds; the unfortunate airman was only allowed back to the block to collect his personnel possessions and to clear his lockers. When he told us that he was being discharged and going home a number of us felt quite envious; the prospect of going back to our families and sleeping in our own beds suddenly became quite appealing. During the first two weeks, a recruit could apply for immediate release and to 'buy himself out' for a payment of £20, but it was not straightforward as was first suggested, and the RAF put a number of obstacles in the way.

There were a number of jokes going around at the time about airmen who wanted to buy themselves out of the service, and an imaginary letter from one such person was pinned to the notice board. It was supposedly written by an airman pleading with his impoverished family: 'Dear Mother, I'm fed up with the air force, so please sell the pig and buy me out!' Her reply was written on a postcard below, 'Dear son, like to help but pig's dead, sold out!'

Applications for the termination of service had to be submitted in writing, and despite the jokes that were going around, I was one of those who applied for an immediate release. I was fed up with my lack of progress and how things were going generally. Within a very short time of putting in my application, I was called to the flight office to be interviewed by my flight commander, Flight Lieutenant Woodward. He asked me why I wanted to leave the RAF and I told him that I thought I did not fit in with the RAF's regime and its way of life. I also said that I was fed up with drill, the bull and the strict disciplinary regime, that I thought it was excessive.

Flight Lieutenant Woodward was hardly sympathetic, but he made it clear that Swinderby was not like a normal RAF station, and that once I had completed my training I would find things very different on other operational stations where discipline would be a lot more relaxed. However, he said that if I still insisted on leaving the service and if I agreed to his terms, I would be given a 48-hour pass over the weekend and allowed to go home. After that, and having had time to think about my decision and discuss it with my family, I could make my mind up and decide if I still wanted to be discharged.

Albeit reluctantly, I agreed, and it was decided that I should leave Swinderby at the end of work at noon on Saturday, and that I should return on Sunday night. The next few days seemed to drag on endlessly, and we spent a great deal of time polishing the brasses on our packs and rubbing Blanco into our webbing belts. We polished our boots in the long lasting service tradition with spit and polish, concentrating mainly on the toe caps until they shone like mirrors. Brasso and shoe polish were parts of our daily life and their pungent smell hung over our room so much, that I reckon we must have been high on the toxic fumes!

Within a short while two things happened that changed my mood and made me question my decision to leave the service. The first one was when our regular instructor Corporal Fagg was replaced by Corporal Stephenson. Corporal Fagg was about to be promoted to the rank of sergeant and he was due for some leave before returning with three stripes on his arm.

Corporal Stephenson was a small, tough looking man, with a completely different personality to Corporal Fagg. He was a member of the RAF Regiment. He had probably served all over the world and his chest full of medal ribbons proved that he was no push over, but it seemed he was happy to let us get on with life in an easy-going fashion. As long as we did our best and did not cause any trouble for him or ourselves, Corporal Stephenson always remained calm and in control.

Sergeant Tewnion continued to take us for drill, but he was normally quite relaxed and did not get flustered when we marched out of step or failed to carry out his instructions, as we often did in the early days. In the more relaxed atmosphere without Corporal Fagg chasing us about, I actually began to enjoy air force life.

The second thing was that on the Thursday at the end of the first week, the clothing store finally issued us with our uniforms and we all began to feel like real airmen instead of freaks with a bad sense of dress. Despite the fact that in most cases the legs of our uniform trousers were too long and the waistbands too wide, wearing them for the first time felt really good and made a very big difference to our sense of pride. I had been informed that because of the uncertainty of whether I was to remain in the RAF, I might not be issued with my uniform. As it happened, I did get it, and I was so pleased that I nearly changed my mind on the spot, but my friend John advised me to take my weekend pass as it had already been arranged, and think about it at home.

The drill session on Saturday morning seemed to go on forever, but finally it ended and I entered the office to collect my first ever leave pass from Sergeant Tewnion. Those who have served in the RAF will be aware that in the service, midnight does not exist. Although I was allowed to leave Swinderby at 1 p.m., technically my leave pass did not begin until 12.01 p.m. on the Saturday night/Sunday morning and it expired at 11.59 p.m. Sunday night. It was not really even a 48-hour pass and in that short time I had to travel to Manchester and back. It was late evening when I got home and by the time I had had something to eat and got to the pub the evening was almost over anyway.

Some of my friends were surprised to see me and only my girlfriend, Christine, knew I was coming home on leave. My best blue uniform raised a few eyebrows and there were lots of jokes about 'Brylcream Boys', while some of those in the bar at the pub tried to take the micky by whistling the Dam Busters tune every five minutes. In the week that I had been away, nothing at all had changed and everything and everyone seemed just as boring as the day that I had left. It did not take me long to remember why I had left to join the RAF in the first place, and my mind was already made up. The jokes and boring conversation of my friends did me a favour; I now knew that I no longer belonged in the town where I had grown up.

The second goodbye in just over a week was even harder than the first, and my mother was convinced that I would be back home again for good within a week. I had not really spoken to her or my father about my intentions, and I could not bring myself to tell her that I had decided to stay in the air force after all.

At Swinderby it felt good to be back, and I was determined to settle down, despite the horror stories that I heard about the first proper Church parade that had been held earlier that day. The CO had inspected the parade, and it had apparently been a shambles, with several airmen being charged for being improperly dressed and several others for minor offences. One recruit was charged with insubordination when he challenged something that the flight commander said to him. I was very grateful that I had missed all the fun!

A few days after my return to Swinderby, I got a letter from my mother telling me that she had sent me a moneygram for £20 to help me buy myself out. I was told that I had to collect it at the post office in Swinderby village, but when I eventually got there I was told it had been forwarded to RAF Swinderby. Despite my repeated enquiries in the office and the guard room, the money never turned up, and £20 was a lot of money to lose in those days. I never told my mother that it had been lost and as I did not use it to buy myself out, she presumed that I had lots of spare cash and subsequently she sent me no more money!

'Bull nights' were held on two or three evenings a week, depending on how the inspections had gone in the morning. Duty lists were posted on the notice boards and every airman in the block was allocated a specific task, such as cleaning the corridors, bathrooms or toilets. Anyone who tried to get out of their assigned duty, or those who failed to complete them properly, were not only disciplined by the senior man but also victimised by the other trainees. The job still had to be done and if an airman failed to complete his allocated task it meant that someone else got lumbered with an extra duty.

For several hours most evenings, our room would be a hive of activity with beds and lockers being lifted from one side of the room to the other, while the floor was swept, polished and bumpered with a big metal hand bumper. For these duties, airmen dressed mainly in shorts or denims and very little else as it was hard, sweaty work. Anyone wanting to leave the room had to get permission from the senior man, and to walk across the floor we had to pad our feet in pieces of old blanket. Once the room had been inspected and approved, everyone's attention would be turned to their own personal kit, and only if time allowed, there would be a mad rush to get down to the NAAFI for the last half hour.

The following morning we would be up very early and start to lay our kit out on our beds. First of all we made bedding up into the dreaded bed pack and laid our kit out in front of it. Everything had its place, as dictated by a large diagram on the wall above the rifle rack. After breakfast there was the most nerve-racking time when we returned to our room and got dressed, ready for inspection. There was an air of fear as our flight commander entered the room accompanied by Corporal Good; as they slowly made their way down the room one could feel the tension mounting. Inevitably, someone always got picked up for something, and it was always a great feeling when it was all over and we could get outside again into the fresh air.

The airfield's vintage wartime red-brick watch tower stood out from more recent additions to the site, although it had probably not been used for its original purpose for over thirty years. A new local control tower had been built in the 1950s and was typical of its period with a glass dome surrounds of a similar design to one that had been built at Waddington.

A lot of the drill that we practised was carried out on the parade ground on the domestic site, but when it rained we drilled on the airfield or in one of the large hangars, of which there six altogether. By 1968, RAF Swinderby was no longer an active airfield, but the runway was kept on a 'Care and Maintenance' basis and the occasional aircraft did land there. If anyone had taken the trouble to tell us about the history of the airfield, or indeed something of the background of Lincolnshire's connections with Bomber Command during the war, I think we would have all felt better about being there.

The hangars where we marched in 1968 had floors stained with ancient patches of oil and the atmosphere in and around them was electric; one could almost sense the presence of those who had served there in the past. There were still a number of old piston engines scattered around, which were probably used for instructional purposes by engineering apprentices. The last of the large Wellington and Lancaster bombers that had flown from Swinderby during the war had been disposed of many years before, but the presence of the past, in whatever form, could still be felt many years later.

The two Polish units, 300 and 301 Squadrons were the first to be based at Swinderby when it opened in August 1940. They had initially been equipped with the obsolete Fairey Battle, but in October of that year they exchanged them for the Wellington 1C, known as the 'Wimpey', in honour of the American cartoonist J. Wellington Wimpey. Both units remained at Swinderby until July 1941, when they moved to Hemswell and were replaced at Swinderby by 50 Squadron. This squadron was equipped with the Handley Page Hampden, but when it moved over to Skellingthorpe in November 1941, Swinderby's operational flying days were over and it reverted to the role of a training station.

1660 Heavy Conversion Unit equipped with the Short Stirling and Avro Lancaster had been based at Swinderby, training crews in the final stage of their training before they moved on to their operational squadrons. Swinderby had been one of three airfields that made up 51 Base, the other two being Winthorpe and Wigsley. After the war, many of the airfields in Lincolnshire were closed down, but Swinderby remained open. In the 1950s, it housed 201 and 204 Advanced Flying Schools, equipped with the Wellington and Mosquito respectively.

Number 8 Flying Training School was one of the last units to regularly use the airfield at Swinderby, and it was equipped with the Vampire T.11. Over the years, a number of its aircraft had been involved in accidents, one of the last ones being in September 1962, when XD448 was abandoned after a bird strike. By 1968, the airfield had closed, although it was kept on Care and Maintenance and the occasional aircraft landed there.

One morning we were marching past a hangar and approaching an area that had at one time had been part of a large dispersal, when a DeHaviland Devon suddenly appeared around the corner, taxi-ing at a considerable

A de Havilland Devon, a military version of the Dove. This aircraft, VP 965, is the same type as VP 960, the aircraft that nearly wiped out a flight of airmen when I was in training at Swinderby, when it unexpectedly appeared around a hangar.

speed. Our corporal shouted 'Break ranks!' but he was too late because we had already scattered in every direction to avoid the whirling propellers and trailing edges of its wings.

The Devon, which was a twin-engined aircraft used primarily for communication duties, was so close to me that all these years later its serial number is still imprinted on my mind: VP960. Someone later claimed that the AOC had been visiting Swinderby, but it is more likely that it belonged to a Southern Communications Squadron and was on a routine flight. With the exception of a small number of Chipmunks that used the airfield at weekends, the Devon was the only active aircraft I saw flying at Swinderby.

During the afternoon of Thursday 18 July, we had our first pay parade. This was a very disciplined affair, and for the first time we paraded in our new best blue uniforms. We were inspected before we were allowed to claim our pay, and then we were lined up in alphabetical order. As my surname name begins with 'B', I was close to the front of the queue. That meant that I did not have much time to see how things were done, which as it happened, was a great disadvantage.

On reaching the front of the queue, each airman had to stand rigidly to attention, state his surname and the last three digits of his service number before smartly saluting the paying officer. Then, swiftly removing his hat with his left hand and picking up his pay from the table with his right hand, he had to put his hat back on and salute for a second time. At that point the airman had to turn sharply about on his heel and march to the back of the line.

Flight Lieutenant Woodward was the paying officer. He was playing everything exactly by the book and very few airmen satisfied him in carrying out the procedure correctly. Those of us who failed were 'bawled out' by him before being sent to the back of queue to start all over again. The parade was something of a shambles and I went around three times before I collected a grand total of £4 10 shillings, my pay that had to last a fortnight. Nobody joined the air force to get rich!

In the early stages of the course, we learned to drill with the Lee Enfield .303 rifle, a very reliable vintage weapon that had performed well during the Second World War. The rifles were kept in the barrack rooms and securely locked to the wall with a single thick chain that ran through all the weapons. Only a Leading Man or a member of the permanent staff was allowed access to the rifles, and they were also responsible for every aspect of their security. Each weapon was numbered and strict records were kept as to who had what weapon. The .303 was only used for drill and for weapons training; the weapon we later used on the range for live firing was the SLR (Self Loading Rifle).

Before being let loose on the firing range, we had to attend classes on weapons training, and in particular we were taught how to use and maintain the SLR. The first thing we were taught was how to load a magazine with its twenty rounds of .762 ammunition, and then how to fit the magazine safely onto the rifle. The most important point that was drilled into us was that the safety catch had to be on 'safe' at all times other than when we were firing the weapon. I was not very keen on some aspects of weapons training and I found the dismantling and re-assembling of the semi-automatic rifle rather confusing. Some of the components never seemed to fit where I knew they should go, and there always seemed to be at least one piece left over. The SLR was prone to gas stoppages and whenever a stoppage occurred we had to find out whether it was being caused by gas or another fault in the assembly.

The 25-yard firing range at Swinderby was closed for de-leading during this period, so we were taken by bus to Waddington to use its facilities. At this time, Waddington housed two units of the Avro Vulcan, numbers 44 and 50 Squadrons. Previously, I had only seen a Vulcan as a dot in the sky ahead of a contrail; to view one close up was very exciting. A small number of them were scattered around the airfield and a few of them were still painted in 'anti-flash' white, while others had already been converted to the low level camouflage scheme. There were not as many aircraft as I might have expected to see at such an important base because the runway at Waddington was being re-surfaced and most of the Vulcans were temporarily based at Scampton and Coningsby.

When we were taken onto the firing range, the noise of engines being run up and other activity on the airfield was a great distraction. We were given strict instructions on range procedure and ordered not to move forward until our names were called out. When my turn came I struggled to sight the rifle because I discovered I could not close my left eye and keep the right one open. This was a great inconvenience; after a brief meeting held between the instructors it was decided that I could fire the rifle left handed. The SLR was not meant to be fired left handed because the empty cartridges flew out across the front of one's face. It was a very unpleasant experience, but one that I would have to repeat at regular intervals.

Back at Swinderby the course progressed quite fast and we were instructed in the procedures concerning nuclear, chemical and biological warfare. We were forced to wear the white paper NBC suits and gas masks, but the exercise seemed so far removed from reality that I do not think anyone took it seriously. It was claimed that if we were contaminated by nerve gas we could inject ourselves with antropene, which might protect us from its full effects. The fact that if a conflict had got to that stage, most of mankind might already have been wiped out was not mentioned by our instructors, and the prospect of such a disaster made it all seem unreal.

To get a sample of what is was like to work in a contaminated atmosphere, we were forced to experience the effects of C.S. gas by entering a small room that had been filled with it. As we walked in, the door was shut behind us and straight away we were ordered to remove our gas mask. Then we had to stand to attention before an NCO, repeat our name and the last three digits of service numbers, before another door opened and we were released. The effect that the gas had on our eyes and ears was very unpleasant, making it an experience that no one wanted to repeat in a hurry! Several recruits felt ill afterwards, and most of us had very bad headaches for the next few days.

There were also lectures on security and we were told in no uncertain terms that we were not to discuss what we did in the RAF with anyone, and that included our family and friends. We were warned that those among us who would eventually end up working in sensitive areas might be targeted by enemy agents or agitators who lived closer to home. The main principle on security was the 'need to know' basis, and that basically meant we did not discuss what we did with anyone unless they had a valid reason for having the information. Likewise, we should never ask anyone else, including our close friends and colleagues, what work they did for the very same reason.

That principle worked well in theory, but the 'hangar doors' were always open, and everyone talked about work in their off-duty time and while having a drink. To complain to each other about what we were asked to do and those senior NCOs and officers that made our life difficult was a way of letting off steam in a system that had few outlets other than the official channels. The best thing was to know who you were talking to and under no circumstances talk to strangers, even those in uniform, about the RAF or your specific role.

A couple of weeks after our arrival at Swinderby, John, my friend who I had first met on the concourse of Manchester Piccadilly Station, was posted out to Boulmer. Because he had already served in the RAF for a number of years, his basic training was cut short; after a short refresher course he was going to continue in his previous role of as an Assistant Fighter Controller. It was a sad moment as we shook hands for the last time. I had a lot to thank him for and he had looked after me very well, especially in his role as Leading Man. I now had an empty bed next to mine, but it was nice to have a bit more space. That was until Corporal Fagg appeared and told me that from now on the recruit on the other side of the bed and I were responsible for keeping it clean. That meant more chores!

There was a distasteful incident involving one recruit in my room, who was found red-handed trying to break into another airman's locker. The airman in question had reported sick that morning but he then sneaked back to our room, where he found himself all alone. Unfortunately for him, when he was right in the middle of committing the act, another airman also returned to the room.

The second airman, one of the Scottish lads who could easily handle himself, realised what the other was up to and a scuffle broke out, during which he overpowered the thief and dragged him to the flight office. There was some confusion over what had happened because the thief wouldn't tell the truth; both airmen were detained in the guard room until the matter was investigated. A subsequent search of the suspect's lockers by the RAF Police revealed a treasure trove of stolen goods that few of us had realised had gone missing! By late evening the innocent airman, our Scottish friend, was back in the room preparing for a Bull Night and we never saw the thief again.

As well as at least two periods of drill every day, we had to endure regular sessions of PT, for which we had to dress in our RAF-issue baggy blue shorts and white t-shirts. In the gym we were made to climb the wall bars then jump from the top onto rubber mats where we then had to do a number of press-ups. Each press-up had to be done with a perfectly straight neck and back otherwise it did not count and we had to start all over again. One of the more sadistic instructors would closely watch what was going on, and if he observed any airman doing press-ups while bending his back he would hit him across the buttocks with his stick.

On some occasions we were made to play a game that involved forming what was effectively a rugby scrum, which got ever bigger as members of the flight ran and jumped on to the backs of the others. The aim was to see how long the pack could stand up; when it collapsed, those at the bottom of the pack got crushed. It was a painful and tiring experience. I preferred the long cross-country runs up the runway and around the perimeter of the airfield, where we passed the burned-out remains of a number of aircraft. It was a more individual and leisurely experience where one could enjoy the fresh air and get some time to one's self.

About half-way through our training we were taken to Sherwood Forest to spend four days under canvas and learn about the practicalities of living in field conditions. All our kit was transported in 3-ton lorries, while, as normal, we travelled in the blue Bedford bus. Fortunately, when we arrived the tents had already been put up and the best part of the camp established and organised. We did, however, have to dig our own latrines, as well as wet and dry pits to bury the huge amount of waste generated by our camp. Cans, bottles and other solids had to be disposed of in the dry pit, while kitchen waste, slops and other liquids went into the wet pit. This was strictly controlled and anyone found putting waste into the wrong pit was in deep trouble.

In each tent four airmen and their camp beds were packed like sardines with very little room to move. The worse thing was that we had no hot or cold running water; it had to be collected from the water bowser in buckets and then boiled in cauldrons on the campfire. There was such a demand for hot water first thing in the morning that we resolved to shave in cold water, and even though it was July, it was not a very pleasant experience.

Subsequently, I began to use my Phillips battery shave, which I also lent out to a couple of lads in my tent for the promise of a beer in return. I knew that it did not give such a close shave to match the RAF's exacting standards expected on parade. Back at Swinderby I had already been warned about my '5 o'clock shadow', and had been ordered that in future I should only wet shave. Under canvas in the forest, things were a little more relaxed, and bit of stubble here and there was tolerated.

If the idea of the camp was to get us used to the hardships of outdoor life, then it failed miserably; within a few days we discovered that a mobile fish and chips van regularly visited the park. The senior NCOs knew about it all the time and probably stuffed their faces with cod and chips every night. They told us about it on the second night in camp and talked about it being our 'treat', but some wise characters had already discovered the van on the first night. It was a welcome change from the typical service rations served up from the field kitchen, consisting mainly of sausages, beans and more beans. Bacon was a rare treat. Whether the beans were to blame or our sweaty socks, the smell in our tent was awful!

On our last day in the forest we took part in an orienteering exercise and were divided up into teams. Team leaders were issued with maps and a compass and the rest of us had to follow their directions. Landmarks such as the Major Oak, where Robin Hood had reputedly hidden, were marked along the route. We did not see any sign of Robin or his Merry Men but there were a lot of odd-looking characters about – most of them were wearing RAF fatigues and looking very lost!

My team argued for most of the way around the course, but at least we completed it and were able to prove it, even though we were among the last to return. Some shysters never ventured far from camp and returned prematurely to claim they had completed the circuit, but unbeknown to them there were spies lurking in the bushes and those who cheated were disqualified.

The final exercise involved an army unit, who were detailed to attack our camp and take as their prize the bell that was hung on a tripod in middle of the camp. The bell was used to rouse us in a morning and was rung at meal times, but on the final night it was the aim of the army to steal it from under very our noses. We were placed on guard at strategic positions around the camp; everyone was aware that the army was coming, either in numbers or under cover. In the early hours of morning there was a disturbance and everyone heard a bell ringing, before it suddenly went quiet again.

It was dark and very few of us had torches, but in the confusion the guards ran off in pursuit of a loud 'clanging sound', failing to check whether the bell was still there or not. The feint worked and they left the bell unguarded so the 'enemy' were able to creep in and steal it. It was rather a pathetic end to what had been not a bad week.

On our return we were happy to be back at Swinderby, and keen to get on and complete our training. The outward-bound camp was probably a turning point for many of us, and the following week we exchanged our yellow cap badges for white ones, indicating that another week's progress had been made. We mastered the skill of getting back into step if we lost our timing; it involved taking the right foot around the back of the left one and making a little skipping movement. It was not an easy thing to learn and a number of airmen ended up on the floor, having tripped themselves up, or more often the unsuspecting airman in front of him. But Corporal Stephenson had a sense of humour and was very patient with those of us, like me, who were slow to learn.

By now, one or two recruits in my flight were beginning to shine, but I was not one of them. Aircraftsman Alan Kerkin was an obvious candidate for a commission because he rose above everybody else, being something of a perfectionist in turn out and drill. Alan's brother was already in the air force as a flying officer in an aircrew role on the Vulcans at RAF Scampton. It was obvious that Alan was destined to follow in his brother's footsteps, but via another route – the ranks. Whether Alan had previously been turned down for a commission we never found out, but it was obvious to all of us that he was a class above everyone else in our flight. His southern accent was clipped and sharp, and although many thought he was something of a snob, I think everyone secretly admired him.

Most evenings we congregated in the NAAFI bar, which appropriately enough was called 'The Gateway Club'. It was the main venue where we met recruits from the other intakes and flights. We sat around and talked about what had happened during the day, while others huddled around the juke box playing the same records over and over again. There was a large Welsh contingent who played Tom Jones's 'Green Green Grass Of Home' so many times that they must have worn it out. There was a fight one night because one group got so fed up with listening to homesick, drunken Welshmen singing along to it, that they repeatedly rejected it on the juke box.

Alcohol was almost always the cause of most trouble, one way or another, and I was far too young to drink legally as I had only had my seventeenth birthday in April 1968. Not long before joining up, I'd had a narrow escape when two policemen interrupted a late night drinking session. I feared that they would discover my age, but as it turned out they were selling tickets for the local Police Ball, and after we had all bought some they joined us for a drink before leaving happily.

A few days later on the night of the Police Ball I was introduced to a chief inspector who, when he heard that I was about to join the RAF, congratulated me and bought me a drink. I have often wondered who would have been most embarrassed if I had been found out, the policeman who sold me the ticket, or the friendly chief inspector who urged me to have an illegal alcohol drink? I did not think that I looked eighteen and I was lucky to get away with it!

The consumption of alcohol under age was considered to be a serious offence and we risked being disciplined and discharged from the RAF with immediate effect if found out. However, we were very rarely challenged to prove our age, even in the NAAFI, despite the fact that it was general knowledge that many of us were under the age of eighteen. Probably because of the close proximity of the number of permanent staff and RAF policemen, there was very little trouble on the station itself, but outside, where there were fewer restraints, it was a different story.

One incident particularly highlighted how seriously the RAF viewed incidents involving members of the public and trouble that occurred off the station. It began one evening when a group of us walked down the road to the Half Way Inn, a local pub on the A46 between Lincoln and Newark. To begin with the atmosphere was pleasant enough, but it was not long before we came under attack with a bit of banter from a few of the locals. The trouble escalated when one of the lads noticed that our hats, which we had left piled up on a table by the door, had been thrown on the floor, and a quick check revealed that some of them were missing.

Among our party that night was a small number of Scottish lads who had been brought up in rough areas of Glasgow; any sensible person would not have wanted to mix it with them. It was they who demanded that the hats should be returned to their owners, but when the request was ignored, the place erupted into chaos. A fight broke out between some of the recruits from my flight and the local yokels who refused to return the hats and other personal possessions. Within minutes, the pub resembled a scene from a John Wayne movie; tables went over, glasses were thrown and broken, and girls screamed as bodies fell in heaps on the floor.

Someone shouted out that landlord had called the police, and those of us that were on the edge of the fray and had not been directly involved, grabbed a hat – any hat from those still left on the table – and ran up the road towards camp. We stopped up the lane several times and waited for the others, but some of the lads, especially the lively Glaswegians, were still in the pub, slowly dismantling it bit by bit, looking for their hats. They eventually got back to camp just before lights out at 10.30 p.m., looking battered and bruised but proud of the fact that they had taught the locals a lesson! Excited chatter went on long after lights out.

Next morning on parade nothing was said immediately, but later on, after roll call and breakfast, we were called back to the billet and paraded again before Flight Lieutenant Woodward. At his side was a civilian, a small stocky man who some of us recognised from our visit to the pub the previous evening. Our flight commander read the Riot Act and introduced the man as the landlord of the Half Way Inn and informed us that he had come to identify those who were responsible for causing damage to his property. The landlord slowly walked among us, but failed to positively recognise anyone although he had his suspicions about a small number of us. Fortunately I was not one of them!

With no positive identification having been made, we were brought to attention again and the flight commander gave us the option that either those responsible for the damage should own up, or all of us would be charged under the training school's policy of joint responsibility. We were given the deadline of 3 p.m. for the guilty parties to admit their part or proceedings would begin. As we were dismissed it went very quiet and everyone shuffled away, before congregating in small groups, muttering to themselves. We were all very nervous about how events would turn out, but we need not have been; within the hour, three of the Scottish recruits admitted their part in the fracas and the rest of us were mightily relieved.

It was a very brave thing to do because they knew that they would be punished severely for letting the RAF down, and more importantly, 7 School of Recruit Training. However, there was considerable pressure on them from other recruits who had taken no part in the affair, and many had never even been to the Half Way Inn. These recruits were unwilling to be implicated in something that had not involved them, and it is possible that someone might have spoken up as most knew who had taken part. We heard later that one of the guilty party had been dismissed from the RAF, while the other two were fined and back-flighted two weeks. That meant that they would have another two weeks in basic training, as well as having their service records blighted.

Despite the fact that we were in the RAF, most of the recruits had never flown before and many of them could not tell the difference between a Spitfire and a London bus. To give us some flying experience we were taken to RAF Scampton for a flight in an Andover, a twin-engined aircraft that had entered RAF service with 46 and 52 Squadrons in December 1966. To my surprise, not only had most of my fellow recruits not flown before, but some were actually scared of flying, and a small number declined the offer of a flight.

Those who did not want to fly had no pressure put on them to do so and they were allowed to remain on the bus while we boarded the Andover. It was the first time I had been on board a service aircraft, and the first thing that I noticed was that the seats were facing the wrong way, towards the rear of the aircraft. This was quickly explained to us by one of the crew who told us that all RAF transport aircraft had rear-facing seats. It was official policy and believed to be a safer practice, but one that would never be tolerated by civilian airlines and fare-paying passengers.

Our flight was supposed to take us over the north of Scotland to view the oil fields that were being developed, but the weather interfered with those plans. It was overcast and wet and so we were flown up the East Coast to Scotland, before we headed back to Scampton. There was nothing to see out of the windows except dense cloud, and after being airborne for an hour-and-a-half we landed back at Scampton.

Before we boarded the coach that would to take us back to Swinderby, our corporal marched us to the main gate and allowed us to view the

Lancaster bomber that acted as its 'Gate Guardian'. We had all heard about the heroics of Guy Gibson and the Dam Busters who had taken off from Scampton in May 1943, and many of my fellow recruits were convinced that this aircraft had taken part in the raid. In actual fact, the Lancaster, serial number R5868, was there for another reason; it had probably flown the highest number of operations of any aircraft of its type. She has been credited with an incredible 137 operations, although there has been some doubt cast upon that claim.

To be able to stand so close to such a large aircraft, one I had only previously read about in papers and magazines, was an incredible experience. Most of us knew that it was such things as this that had inspired us to join the air force, and we felt very proud to be there.

From that moment in time, I began to respect the airmen who had flown in the heavy bombers such as the Lancaster, and many years later I actually met a former senior NCO who had flown two sorties in R5868 with 467 Squadron from Waddington during 1944. Warrant Officer Thorpe was the rear gunner in his crew, and although his first sortie in R5868 was on an exercise, his second flight on 28 June was an operational sortie bombing objectives around Cherbourg.

In 1993, many years after the Lancaster had been moved to the RAF Museum at Hendon, Warrant Officer Thorpe's grandson was on a visit to the museum when he saw a notice requesting information from anyone whose family or friends had flown on R5868. The museum was trying to confirm the number of operations that the Lancaster had completed and wanted former aircrew to check their log books. When Mr Thorpe heard about the appeal, he got in touch with Hendon and after his log book had been inspected and checked against the squadron records, his sortie in the Lancaster was confirmed. The operation of 28 June was one of those missing from the records, and it was the final one to confirm that R5868 had completed 137 sorties.

All our drill was now aimed at getting us prepared for the passing out parade two weeks hence, and by now we had exchanged the clumsy .303 rifles for the SLR that was held in the right hand under its wooden stock. It was a lot easier to drill with, although when we began to practice with fixed bayonets a recruit in my flight managed to impale his hand. It happened while we were presenting arms on the move, and somehow the airman in question, Duncan, swung his left arm over a bit too enthusiastically and hit the bayonet. He was taken off to the medical centre while the rest of us continued. Corporal Stevenson viewed the incident as an occupational hazard.

Prior to us becoming the senior flight, a disco and party was thoughtfully arranged for us, which included a visit from the WAAFs who were based at RAF Spittelgate, near Grantham. Like Swinderby, Spittelgate was a former airfield that had been closely associated with 39 Squadron, which had occupied the site from 1923 to 1928, flying the DH 9. When the squadron moved out to India, the airfield closed down; by 1968, Spittelgate was the Recruit Training Centre for the Women's Auxiliary Air Force, the female equivalent of Swinderby.

It was noticeable that in the days leading up to the WAAF's visit, many of my fellow recruits did not drink any of the tea, coffee or fruit juice that was on offer in the mess. There had been talk about it being loaded with bromide ever since we arrived at Swinderby and the wiser and more experienced airmen had refused to drink it. During our official 48-hour pass, I had had an experience with my girlfriend that was probably the result of bromide, but as I was fairly naïve at the time and I refused to believe that such things could happen! That our drinks were spiked is now beyond doubt and the practice was common knowledge among those who served during the war.

The party that was held in the NAAFI was a fairly wild affair and I seem to remember the records of Arthur Brown's 'Fire' and July Driscoll's 'Wheels On Fire' being played very loud over and over again. The girl's arrived at about 7 p.m., and the fun began immediately with some airmen pairing off with WAAFs almost automatically. What struck me and a few other airmen in my flight was how big and ugly some of them were – in their ill-fitting baggy uniforms they looked like battleships.

The few good looking girls got snapped up almost as soon as they stepped off the bus, while the others milled around looking for an opportunity to pounce on any airmen who talked to them. I had one close encounter with a WAAF who would not have been out of place in a cage at Chester Zoo. After that experience I hid away in dark corner with a few others, quietly drinking beer. We opened the hangar doors and talked shop all night, trying to ignore the drunken debauchery that was going on all around us. After couple of hours the party got very lively and there was plenty of it to ignore!

The following morning everyone had hangovers, but that did not stop talk of various sexual encounters of the previous evening and other lewd tales that quickly circulated around the block. It was a Sunday morning and as a special concession we were excused parade, however, two prominent members of our flight had not slept in their beds and everyone was wondering what had happened to them.

Rumours began to spread that they had last been seen with a couple of WAAFs and had been talking about taking them out on the town for a drink in Lincoln. It was also claimed that the two airmen had been seen leaving camp. By late Sunday night they had still not arrived back at Swinderby and they were still absent when we paraded at 7.30 a.m. on the Monday morning. By that time we knew that they were in big trouble and when they finally turned up at lunchtime more rumours abounded as to their ultimate fate.

It was confirmed later that they had hitched a ride to Spittelgate and spent the Sunday with the two WAAFs they had met the night before. Going there they had been very lucky in getting a lift, but coming back in the early hours of a cold Monday morning, they had been less fortunate, and had had to walk much of the way. They were both very tired and for various reasons they had probably not slept properly since the Friday night. Regardless of that, they said they'd had a great time and had no regrets.

They were both charged with being Absent Without Leave (AWOL) and at their hearing in front of the flight commander they were given seven days 'Jankers'. That meant they had to report to the guard room at 7 a.m. in full kit and again at 10 p.m. for inspection by the orderly officer. At some point during the punishment they probably did regret they had ever met the WAAFs.

In preparation for our passing out parade, we were instructed in ceremonial drill. In particular, we practised the Slow March, which proved to be one of the most difficult movements to perform. If an airman was out of step or got out of rhythm it was obvious to any observers because of the slowness of the movement. The right foot had to be fully extended, as did then the left foot, and between each step it felt like our legs were hanging in the air. The timing had to be exact, otherwise the whole thing could easily break down, as happened a few times in practice, when a couple of my colleagues ended up on the floor.

The final week of training turned out to be good fun and for the first time we were finally allowed to wear the badges on our hats without any coloured discs behinds them. We also had the special privilege of being allowed into the private bar area of the Gateway Club in the NAAFI, and on a few occasions we were actually joined in the evenings by Corporals Fagg and Stephens and Sergeant Tewnion. The atmosphere was friendly and they addressed us as in a civilised fashion as airmen, and we addressed them politely as 'corporal' or 'sergeant'. Any attempt to use first names would not have been tolerated by our instructors.

The culmination of our six weeks basic training was put to the test on 15 August, when at 10.20 a.m. exactly, under the eye of the parade commander, Flight Lieutenant P. Woodward, we marched onto the parade ground. There were a total of four flights taking part in the parade, with two forming the Review Squadron and two backing up as the Support Squadron. The first review squadron flight was Number 1, lead by Flight Lieutenant Neal. My flight was Number 2 lead by Flying Officer McCulloch, with Sergeant Tewnion as his senior NCO. We marched to music played by the Number 1 Regional Band, and the wonderful marching tunes added extra swagger to our appearance.

My mother and father travelled from Manchester to Swinderby, spending the whole night on a train, in what they recalled was a very slow and cold journey. As a surprise they had brought along my girlfriend, Chirstine, who I had not seen for several weeks; I am not so sure that she was very enthusiastic about being there. From the parade ground I looked out for my mother and father in the crowd, but the crowd of people were all a bit of a blur as I had to concentrate on the matter in hand.

Everything went according to plan and at 10.30 a.m. the reviewing officer, Group Captain Edward Peter Landon DFC, the commanding officer of RAF Bassingbourn, took his place on the podium. The group captain was a veteran who had flown in Bomber Command with 462 Squadron (Australian) and had been awarded the DFC in January 1944 while serving as a flying officer in the Royal Australian Air Force. He had flown the Halifax Mk II and had operated in various theatres, but mainly in the Middle East where 462 was based for much of the war.

There were a lot of anxious moments as he slowly made his way along the ranks, stopping occasionally to talk to airmen. There was quite a stiff breeze and a photograph taken at the time shows that the trousers of most airmen on parade were flapping wildly. I was positioned second from the end, next to the marker on the back row. Standing rigidly to attention with my SLR in my right hand, I awaited Group Captain Landon's inspection. He stopped to speak to a recruit two rows up from me, and as it happened, I got no more than a cursory glance when he walked past to complete the review.

The group captain presented the Efficiency Trophy, the Sport's Cup, the Drill Cup and Certificates of Merit. Number 5 Flight won the Efficiency Trophy, but the other two went to 2 Flight. Aircraftsman Kerkin was awarded a Certificate of Merit, as we all knew he would, with the other one going to A. C. Williams. As the parade drew to a close there was a flypast by three

Canberras from Bassingbourn, and everyone's eyes were drawn towards the sky as they swooped across the airfield very low.

With the sound of the jet's engines fading into the distance, the band began to play the Royal Air Force Swinderby March as the recruits of the Support Squadron began to march off the parade ground. Along with the crowd, we were encouraged to sing along to the music, but most of us were just too excited and so mimed the words instead!

> When we join the Royal Air Force
> We are sent to Swinderby
> Meet the corpral and the sergeant
> They politely tell us what to do
>
> We draw our kit and get our hair cut
> Lots of drill and GDT
> It seems a long way to pass out day
> We're the boys of the SRT

My passing out parade at RAF Swinderby on 15 August 1968. I am second from the right with perfectly straight trousers, while those of other airmen were blowing in the breeze. The reviewing officer was Group Captain Landon DFC from RAF Bassingbourne.

We go left right left right
As we march behind the band
And in six weeks we pass out
The smartest in the land

Swing along at Swinderby
The latest in air force blue
We are displaying every day
What air force training can do

Dressed the best we're marching past in line
And we march in column too
And now that we have made pass out parade
We pass the torch to you

After marching off the parade ground we were all in a hurry to meet up with our families and friends who had watched us parade and pass out. However, before we did that, we had an important ritual to carry out back in our room at the block. For six weeks we had polished the brown lino floor every morning and night with hand bumpers, and by the time of our passing out it shone like glass. We had been tipped off that a new entry was due later on that day and our room was to be occupied again within a few hours of our departure. It had been intimated by our corporal that it was not the done thing for a new flight to inherit all the hard work put in by their predecessors, and that the floor should be 'trashed'.

Without any more prompting, we ran into the room and skidded along the floor, digging the studs of ours boots as deeply into the lino as we could. There was a frenzy of destruction with a dozen or so of us running up and down the room, pulling beds and lockers across the floor to add to the scratches and marks. Within a few minutes the lino had lost its gloss and faded into an ugly brown mass, scarred by our efforts and in much need of renovation. With the job done we tidied up the room, cleared our lockers of our last personal possessions, picked up our holdalls, and went to meet our families.

We were given a week's leave, in which time we were to be informed by telegram of which station we would next be posted to. A few days after I arrived home, I received the telegram ordering me to report to RAF Gaydon in Warwickshire. I did not have a clue where it was. The next day I received a railway warrant for the journey from Manchester to Leamington via Birmingham, but I was still none the wiser.

CHAPTER 3

RAF Gaydon

My next posting should have been to Shawbury to learn my trade at the Central Air Traffic Control School, but because a course was not readily available, I was detached to RAF Gaydon in Warwickshire. After spending nearly a week at home on leave, it was hard to make the break again, but on 21 August I made the long train journey from Manchester to Birmingham New Street, then from Snow Hill Station I caught another very slow train to Lemington, and from there, finally a taxi to RAF Gaydon.

The only thing I found remotely reminiscent of Swinderby at Gaydon was the Station Warrant Officer (SWO), who was a Polish senior NCO that I first met when I reported to the guard room on my arrival. He shouted at me in garbled English to 'smarten yourself up and get a haircut', but because of his strong accent, I could hardly understand what he was saying. However, I soon realised that if I managed to avoid the attention of the SWO there was not much else to worry about; this was an operational station where discipline was almost non-existent.

I was billeted in a large wooden hut that had about ten beds down each side, but other than that set pattern, there was no order of things. The room mainly accommodated firemen from the RAF Regiment, and it was untidy and dirty, with an overwhelming smell of sweaty socks and tobacco. I was the source of some amusement when I arrived because nobody knew why I was there, and although most occupants were friendly enough to begin with, some resented having to move things around and give up their space to provide me with a bed and lockers. While it was claimed that I was a still only a 'sprog' with the ink on my Form 1250 ID card barely dry, the firemen of the RAF were mainly veterans, many of whom had recently returned from active service in Libya or Aden.

Situated on the A41 to the south of Warwick, Gaydon was one of those RAF airfields that had passed me by, and I knew little or nothing about its history. During my detachment there, it was the home of Number 2 Air Navigation School, equipped with the twin-engined Vickers Varsity, better known as the 'Flying Pig'. It was a small, squat aeroplane, fitted with two Bristol Hercules piston engines similar to those that had powered the mighty Halifax bomber during the war. It was a more modern version of the Vickers Valetta T3 Tail Dragger, which had been taken out of RAF service at Gaydon shortly before I arrived.

At Gaydon student navigators underwent initial training that lasted eight months, and in that time they completed 28 hours of elementary exercises, before going on to complete another 28 hours of basic training. After they had successfully completed a complicated solo-navigation exercise, they passed on to Number 1 Air Navigation School at Stradishall. There they were streamed, and those who were destined for transport aircraft would receive further training on the Varsity, while those marked down for fast jets would train on the Hawker Siddley Dominie, a military version of the twin-engined HS 125.

Because nobody was expecting me to arrive at Gaydon, I was passed on from Station Headquarters (SHQ) to the General Duties (GD) section, and then back to SHQ, before someone decided that I should be sent to the control tower. Before I could report to the control tower, I was informed that I had to 'officially arrive', which meant reporting to virtually every section on the station to get my blue card signed.

At the GD Flight, I again fell foul of the ill-tempered SWO, but I collected another signature before going on to the bedding store, the clothing store and the medical centre. The list of sections I had to visit seemed endless, but eventually I got all the necessary signatures to confirm that I had officially arrived. It was my first experience of the RAF's complicated bureaucratic arrivals procedure, but it would not be my last.

At some point during the day I reported for duty in the control tower and I met the sergeant in charge of administration. He took me to the office and explained that there was nothing for me to do except to observe what went on, and get some experience before I went to Shawbury. I was shown around the various positions and given a rough idea of what each assistant and controller did during their shift. With the exception of a brief glimpse inside the tower at Manchester Airport, this was my first real look around a working control tower, and I was impressed by the radar and technology inside the blacked-out approach room.

I reported to the control tower again the next morning, but there was a different atmosphere to the previous afternoon, and it was obvious that I was in the way. Someone suggested that, as I had nothing better to do, I should make a 'brew'; this was another first, because I had never made tea before on such a large scale. I had made pots of tea for my mother and father, but never for so many people, all of whom wanted something different: with sugar, no sugar, and even tea without milk. There were also orders for white coffee, black coffee, with sugar, without sugar, and I was very confused and clearly out of my depth!

The teapot was a huge metal urn and I had no idea how many spoonfuls of tea I should put in it to make the brew. In the end I counted the number of those wanting tea, which was approximately twenty, and decided that would be near enough. Before I could do anything I had to find and collect all the teacups and wash them up. I put plenty of washing up liquid in the bowl and washed them all up before I even began with making the tea or coffee.

By now one or two people were beginning to complain about how long it was taking me, and I felt quite harassed and under pressure. Throwing the tea in the pot without warming it up, I decided to get the chore over with as soon as possible. I had never made coffee before and so that was even more of a hit and miss affair, and I fear I may have used a dessert spoon instead of a teaspoon to make a very strong brew.

I eventually took the cups around on a tray, first into the approach room and then up to local control where the senior air traffic controller, a squadron leader, was talking to some other officers. He asked for a cup with two sugars and I politely gave him the appropriate cup, but I had barely turned my back when I heard him coughing and spluttering.

'Airman ... how many damn sugars have you put in this?' he demanded to know.

'Two, Sir,' I replied rather nervously.

'Well you'd better learn to count, laddy ... because it tastes like you've emptied the whole damn sugar bowl!'

By the time I got back down stairs the admin sergeant was waiting for me with another tray full of cups of tea and coffee that had hardly been touched.

'Didn't do very well did you, son?' he said. 'I think you'd better get off to the mess and have an early lunch,' adding, as an afterthought, 'Don't hurry back ... in fact, we'll see you on Monday morning. Oh and by the way! Next time you make a brew – a piece of good advice – I suggest that you let them put their own sugar in!'

That suited me fine and I was glad to get away from the tower. The only problem was that I knew I would have to spend the weekend on camp with nothing to do and nowhere to go. I had very little money, no real friends or anyone that I knew for company or social contact. It was not a prospect that I relished.

After spending Friday night in the company of the hooligans who occupied my barrack hut, I decided that I had to get away from it, whatever the cost! It was unbearable with the Rock Apes coming in at various times and shouting drunken abuse at those who were already asleep. The lights were switched on and off repeatedly and I was disturbed for most of the night by the sound of someone vomiting. To keep out of trouble I decided to keep my head down and just pretend to be asleep, but I promised myself in the cold light of dawn that I had to get away from the mad house.

On Saturday morning I began trying to hitch a lift on the main road outside the guard room, and it was not long before someone stopped and gave me a ride into Leamington Spa. It was not a particularly great distance from camp and I had to wait some time before anyone stopped again, but I quickly learned that my best chances were on the more isolated roads away from the town centre. I had a very lucky break when the driver of the next vehicle that stopped told me he was going all the way to Sheffield; within a couple of hours I was only 60 miles from home.

My spirits dropped when my journey came to an end and I had to get out of a warm car into the cold damp air and walk through the dank, miserable streets of Sheffield. It was very quiet except for the crowd that I could hear in the distance, cheering on Sheffield Wednesday at Hillsborough. Somehow I made it to the bottom of the A57, but by then I began to feel very tired. I stuck my thumb out every time I heard a vehicle approaching and eventually a car towing a caravan appeared, but although the driver glanced in my direction it drove straight past me. Then I saw the brake lights come on and the driver tooted his horn before he stopped a hundred or so yards up the road.

My saviour urged me to get in and told me he was going to Blackpool via Glossop and Manchester, driving along the A6. I could not believe my luck again! He was very chatty and told me that his son was in the RAF and he always stopped to pick up servicemen hitching lifts if he could. In the end he was true to his word and he went out of his way to drop me off on the A666 in Pendlebury, almost right outside my parents' house. It had taken just three lifts to travel over a hundred miles and I was home by 6.30 p.m.

I was only home for one night but when I visited the pub later that evening I met Dave, a friend whose family had just moved to Bicester, where his father had got a job on the RAF station that was the home of 27 Maintenance Unit. It was only a short distance from Gaydon and Dave told me that he went back home to Salford every Friday night by car and returned early every Monday morning. It was another very lucky connection, although I was not able to make the journey every weekend.

Sometimes we stopped over in Bicester for a drink and I was surprised to see that the town was full of large American cars such as Cadilacs, Buicks and Mustangs. Dave explained to me that most of them belonged to American servicemen and their families that were based in the local area. The majority of them came from Upper Heyford where the USAAF's Third Air Force was based. From there flew the F 100 Super Sabre, F 101 Voodoo, and the more up to date F 4 Phantom. The town was a popular 'watering hole' for the Americans and it catered for their every need.

When I reported back to the control tower on Monday morning the sergeant called me into the office and told me that I was being transferred to Operations, because it was thought that my skills, especially those concerned with making a brew, would be better appreciated there. The sergeant took me down to the operations room and left me in the company of Senior Aircraftsman Keith Barclay. Keith was a very pleasant man and from the very beginning he made me feel welcome. He allowed me to shadow him so that I found out what went on in the operations room in my own time without any pressure.

As on any RAF station, the air operations centre was the hub around which everything else worked. It had to be informed about any details concerning sorties flown by Number 2 ANS Varsities and visiting aircraft. Flight plans were filed there and details of aircraft movements were received from the control tower via a 'squawk box'. Take-off and landing times and other details such as an aircraft becoming 'TOG' – with a Technical Problem on Ground – were recorded on a perspex board with chinagraph pencil. However, despite being made to feel more welcome, as a lowly untrained airman there was little for me to do except make the tea and answer the occasional telephone call.

Making a brew in the operations room was not such a problem as in the control tower as there were normally only three or four people to cater for, including the two regular operations officers, Flight Lieutenants

Brearley and Edwards. Having just left basic training, I still viewed officers as gods, but they put me at ease and on one occasion asked me about my flying experience. I told them about my numerous flights in Vanguards and Viscounts but when they heard that I had never flown in a piston-engined aircraft they said they would soon put that right!

Corporals were still 'Tin Gods' in my mindset, and one in particular, Corporal Roger Darling, began to make my life quite unpleasant. He did not work in the operations room all the time, and I think his main position was in Flight Planning next door to the operations room. However, when he entered the operations room he would pick me up over something and tell me off in a thoroughly unpleasant way. I tried to avoid him but it was almost impossible. But I think Keith noticed what was going on and had a word with him.

During the evenings there was not a lot to do on the station, but there was a station cinema that I visited on several occasions. One of the films that I remember seeing there was 'Billion Dollar Brain' with Michael Cain playing the reluctant Cockney spy, Harry Palmer. I didn't understand what it was all about, and having seen the film a hundred times since, I still don't get the plot! However, as on most RAF stations, the cinema was a cheap way to spend an evening – what was showing never seemed to matter.

Another way of spending an evening was by working on Gaydon's radio station. They broadcast music, station news and gossip from 6 p.m. each evening to the domestic site. It was piped through the station's tannoy system and could be heard in the billets, the NAAFI and the Church Army Centre. Radio stations like the one at Gaydon were a feature of most large RAF bases, and they provided a local centre where airmen and officers could get in touch and have a request played or information broadcast relating to either operational matters or personal affairs.

Only experienced radio station staff were allowed to play the records and broadcast on the air; my duties involved cataloguing records, putting them away when they had been played, and answering the telephone. All the same, it was an interesting experience that gave me heightened ambitions of working as a disc jockey on a pirate radio station or even at the BBC. Hanging on the wall there was a large photograph of Simon Dee, who at the time was a very popular radio and television personality. Word had it that Simon Dee had served at RAF Gaydon, and had actually begun his career on the radio station. I think that was just someone's fantasy because I understand that he never actually served in the RAF. The voice of the then 33-year-old DJ was the first to be heard on the air from Radio Caroline in March 1964, and he later had his own show on BBC Television. As a pirate radio DJ, I do not think Simon Dee would have been given a good reception at an RAF station!

Other than the radio station, for me at least, there were few places to go. The Church Army, however, was a popular place during the evenings to socialise and have a bite to eat. The opportunities to get away off camp were few and far between; one needed a car to get any reasonable distance, as the bus service to Leamington from outside the camp gates was quite limited. Just occasionally someone would ask me if I wanted to join them for a drink. The normal destination was the Malt Shovel, a small pub just up the road in the village. It displayed lots of photographs of crews and aircraft that had visited the station over the years, and had close associations with RAF Gaydon. I spent a number of pleasant evenings there.

Through a civilian MT driver who regularly visited the operations centre, I got to know quite a bit about Gaydon's history, as he not only worked there but was a local man who was proud of its his roots. He told me that RAF Gaydon had opened on 13 June 1942 as a satellite of Number 12 Operational Training Unit (OTU), which was based at Chipping Warden and flew the Vickers Wellington.

Gaydon had also been used by 22 OTU, based at Wellebourne, when its runways were being repaired in 1943, and a number of operational sorties were flown from there. When flying training ceased at Gaydon in July 1945, it was still under the control of Wellesbourne in 23 Group, and later it housed 3 Glider Training School and a Glider Instructor Flight. In 1946, Gaydon was put on a Care and Maintenance basis under the control of 21 (P) Advanced Flying Unit, and there was very little activity.

In 1953, Gaydon was selected as a V-Bomber base. The whole airfield was reconstructed, with a new 9,000-foot runway that was laid down on farmland to the south-west. The station did not open again until 1 March 1954, when it came under the control of 3 Group Bomber Command, but it was not until January 1955 that 138 Squadron was formed there – the very first unit to be equipped with the Vickers Valiant. However, 138 Squadron's time at Gaydon was quite short; in July 1955, after working up to operational capability, it moved to RAF Wittering. It was replaced by 543 Squadron, equipped with the Valiant and Canberra T4, but that squadron in turn left for Wyton in November.

On 2 October 1962, a Victor from 232 Operational Conversion Unit, XA934, crashed into a wood shortly after taking off from Gaydon; three of its crew were killed. The crew had tried to abandon the aircraft after an engine failure on take-off, which was then quickly followed by two others, but only the co-pilot, Flight Lieutenant Gwinnel, survived. My friend the MT driver claimed he had been among the first on the scene, and he described the carnage that he found on his arrival at the crash site. It had happened six years ago, but the incident was as fresh in his mind as if it had happened the day before.

When I arrived at Gaydon, the station was preparing for an open day to celebrate the 'Battle of Britain Week', when the public was admitted to celebrate the 50th Anniversary of the founding of the Royal Air Force. In the week preceding the event, many different types of aircraft arrived at Gaydon so that their crews could familiarise themselves with the airfield and practice their routines. From the United States there were various versions of the F 100 Sabre and F 4 Phantom, while the RAF itself contributed with most types it had in service, but the Canberra and Lightning were particularly well represented. Being in Operations, I got to meet many of the pilots and crews of the aircraft, and on one occasion, in a practice run before the open day, I managed to get a flight in a Wessex helicopter.

There was to be a mock battle on the airfield involving a number of soldiers who were based at Kineton, a huge underground munitions depot that was just down the road from Gaydon. The soldiers were going to drop onto the airfield by abseiling from the helicopter to attack an 'enemy' position while others were to be landed in and around the fort by helicopter. The Wessex helicopter that I flew in was carrying armed troops to various tactical points on the airfield.

It was my first flight from Gaydon and also my first ever flight in a helicopter, but it was to be remembered for all the wrong reasons, mainly soldiers vomiting at various stages! It started almost as soon as we got airborne when the first of the dozen or so soldiers on board began being sick, and the loadmaster had to get the pilot to make an impromptu landing. As we progressed around the airfield, dropping them off at various locations, it continued, with some of the soldiers being sick as soon as they jumped out, while others could not last that long and brought it up inside the door, much to the dismay of the loadmaster.

After dropping them all off, we had to fly and hover around for a while, but we did get the opportunity to watch the mock battle on the ground with a variety of explosions taking place in the cardboard forts. We then went around the various pick-up points, collected all the troops up again and dropped them off back at the dispersal. By that time the helicopter smelt like a Turkish wrestler's jockstrap, but despite everything, it was quite an exciting hour or so, and I went back to the operations room feeling that I had reached a new stage in my fledgling career in the RAF.

On the days prior to the open day, we watched many of the crews practising their flying displays from the open doors of Flight Planning, behind the operations building. One performance that I will never forget was by a Canberra that performed a series of spectacular manoeuvres over the airfield, concluding in a loop from a remarkably low height. It seemed an incredible manoeuvre for an aircraft of that size to perform; at the top of the loop the Canberra seemed to hang upside down for ages before swooping down to earth again.

One American pilot standing next to me muttered loudly, 'Jesus, what a great manoeuvre ... if I was up there I think I'd need a whole box of toilet roll!' His sentiments were shared by other onlookers, raising a smile on the faces of a number of RAF officers who overheard him.

To avoid yet another confrontation with the Polish SWO and being ordered to 'Get a haircut!' I started to sneak into the camp through a hole that I found in the fence. It was a well-known unofficial means of entry into the base, via a path around the back of the main guard room and through a small coppice. The path passed close to an old green hangar that stood isolated at the edge of the perimeter; by its shabby appearance, it appeared to be quite neglected and forgotten. However, on one occasion I decided to sneak a look inside, and what I saw totally surprised me. Through the small dusty window, I could see some of the finest rare vintage aircraft in the country!

Among the collection were a number of wartime aircraft including an Me 262, a Focke Wolf 190, a rocket-powered Me 163 and a Japanese Mitsubishi Zero. My instinct told me that these aircraft were the genuine article and not replicas. It seemed that I had stumbled across a treasure trove, but I didn't want to be caught in the area so I stealthily moved away and told no one what I had found. Much later I learned that the aircraft were being stored at RAF Gaydon while they waited to be moved to the new RAF Museum at Hendon. What I had stumbled across that day was immensely precious to the nation.

On Saturday 14 September, the great day of 'Meet the Royal Air Force At Home' took place. Although the flying display did not begin until 1.45 p.m., the gates opened to the public at 10 a.m. Entry by a car cost 10/– (50p), and 40/– (£2) for a full coach load. With the exception of a few people from the local villages, most people arrived in cars or buses and travelled from all over the West Midlands. It was a brilliant fine sunny day to start with, and ideal conditions for those both performing and watching the air displays.

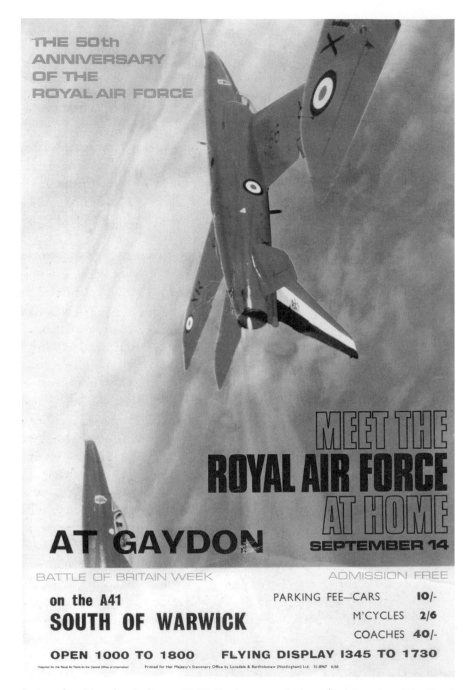

Poster advertising the air show at RAF Gaydon to mark the 50th anniversary of the Royal Air Force. It features three Gnats of the Red Arrows.

The highlight of the afternoon's display was, as it still is today at any air show, the Red Arrows, a team with a distinguished heritage. The RAF's first jet aerobatic team was made up of three Vampires from 72 Squadron, based at Odiham in 1947. The team was lead by Squadron Leader M. Lyne, and it operated up to 1950, by which time it had seven Vampires. The first jet aerobatic team to trail smoke was a five-ship display team of Vampires from 54 Squadron in 1953. In 1955, four of 54 Squadron's Hawker Hunters formed a team called the 'Black Knights', and in 1956, 111 Squadron used four Hunters in a display team. After 111 Squadron increased the number of aircraft in its team to seven, the following year they became known as the 'Black Arrows'. These were the foundations on which the 'Red Arrows' built its reputation.

The team had been formed in 1964 and were originally part of 4 Flight Training School based at Valley. Equipped with the Folland Gnat, the display team was originally called the 'Yellowjacks', and only became known as the Red Arrows the following year, under the leadership of Squadron Leader Ray Hannah. At Gaydon it was the first time I had seen a live Red Arrows display, and it was hard to believe that I was able to get so close to its aircraft and mingle with the pilots.

The team for 1968, under the leadership of Squadron Leader Hannah was Flight Lieutenants D. A. Bell, D. A. Smith, P. R Evans, F. J. Hoare, R. Booth, J. T. Kingsley, I. C. H. Dick and R. B. Duckett. The team manager was Squadron Leader L. G. Wilcox. Displaying at Gaydon, their aircraft were XR540, XR986, XZ987, XS111 and XR991–XR996. These were the same ten Gnats that had displayed at Abingdon in June for the Royal Review.

Among these aircraft on static display was the Meteor 1 prototype, serial number DG202, and Supermarine Swift WK281. The Me 262 (112372) that I had recently observed in the old green hangar was also on static display. There was also another Meteor from Boscombe Down, WS 838, which was painted in an all yellow colour scheme. The prototype Jet Provost XD674 was also on static display, only because by that time it had been relegated to an instructional airframe. With its spindly undercarriage legs, Jet Provost XD674 was hardly recognisable as the RAF's popular basic trainer, one of the most common types in service.

As well as a strong vintage element on display, there were also modern aircraft like the forerunner to the Harrier, a P1127, XP976. A Tiger Moth and Leopard Moth gave solo flying displays, but the cavalcade of vintage aircraft had to be abandoned when the weather suddenly deteriorated during the afternoon.

At one point it rained so hard that a Spitfire that was due to give a flying display, PS853, sunk in the mud up to its axles and had to be towed away. The Spitfire Mk XIX had been built in January 1945 and delivered to the Central Photographic Unit at Benson.

In June 1957, PS853 became part of the Battle of Britain Memorial Flight, which had been formed that very year at Biggin Hill; it had been flown there by the wartime flying ace, Group Captain Johnny Johnson. In 1960 it was decided that the aircraft should be grounded, and so it became the Gate Guardian at West Raynham. Fortunately it was kept in flying condition and in 1964 it once again joined the Memorial Flight. Just the very sight of the Spitfire brought back wartime memories for many older visitors; it was one of the star attractions.

Towards the end of the event I was conscripted to carry out duties as a waiter in the hospitality tent where many people had congregated to get

Spitfire Vb AB910 that entered service with 222 Squadron but later served with 130, 133, 242, 416, 402 and 507 Squadrons. It is best known as the aircraft that took LACW Margaret Horton for an unexpected flight on 4 April 1945 when she was hanging on to the tail. The pilot, Flight Lieutenant Cox, thought that the aircraft was not responding to the controls and landed immediately, so Margeret Horton survived to tell the tale. The aircraft is seen here on a visit to Manston shortly after being delivered to the Battle of Britain Memorial Flight.

out of the rain. None of the aircrew were drinking for obvious reasons, but many of them came in to seek out their friends and family or to sample the cuisine. Dressed in a white monkey suite, my job was to mingle among the guests, who were mainly officers, and offer them champagne and nibbles. It was all too brief a moment in time, and by the early evening the aircraft began to depart, including the Red Arrows, who were based just a short distance away at Kemble.

When the last of the aircraft departed on Monday morning, it left the airfield looking very empty and everybody in Operations and Flight Planning felt very flat after such a busy weekend. However, things brightened up again on Wednesday when I was invited by Flight Lieutenant Edwards to fly with him in a Varsity to St Athan near Cardiff in South Wales. It surprised me when I was told that I had to wear a parachute harness, an uncomfortable piece of equipment that fastened under one's crotch. I was instructed in the use of a parachute and shown where they were stowed, but if I had been ordered to jump I do not think I would have done so willingly!

As I climbed up the short metal ladder into the fuselage, the strange aroma of oil, kerosene and leather hit me, and within a minute or so, the Bristol Hercules engines coughed into life. There was no doubt that this was a real aeroplane and it felt very different to anything I had experienced before. As we taxied out to the runway there were lots of squeaks as Flight Lieutenant Edwards applied the brakes to turn. There were other noises from the hydraulics, and the aircraft rumbled, rather than rolled, along the taxiway. After final checks at the end of the runway, full power was applied and the aircraft shook violently as Flight Lieutenant Edwards guided it, with Flight Lieutenant Brearley's left hand on the throttles.

Keith Barclay was also on board; he occupied the right-hand seat shortly after take-off and appeared to be very competent at the controls. Flight Lieutenant Brearley stood behind Keith and monitored what he was doing, while I stood beside him trying to see the ground below through the windscreen. I had a headset on and so I was able to hear what was being said over the radio, but the noise and vibration was overwhelming, as was the very sensation itself.

As we approached Cardiff, Flight Lieutenant Brearley asked me if I was interested in rugby and he pointed ahead to a large stadium that soon disappeared beneath the aircraft. 'Cardiff Arms Park,' he shouted above the roar of the engines. We did a wide orbit of the stadium before setting course for St Athan a short distance away to the west. Flight Lieutenant Brearley took his seat for the landing and Keith joined me, seated in the back and secured. We were delivering a part for another Varsity that had landed there and had become unserviceable, so we were not on the ground very long before the engines started up again and we took off for the return flight to Gaydon.

It was all over too quickly, but the following day I made two more flights to Oakington and Pershore and I was beginning to enjoy myself. Then on the same day I was told that my course at Shawbury would begin the following week and I was ordered to report to the general office and clear the station the next day. It was all a bit of a rush, running around with my blue chitty and trying to get the appropriate signatures while avoiding bumping into the SWO at the same time.

On my last night I went to the baths in Leamington Spa with Keith Barclay, Flight Lieutenant Brearley, and some members of their families. In my eagerness to get into the water, I ran from the changing rooms and dived straight in without realising that it was the shallow end. The water was only 3 feet deep and I cracked my head on the bottom and nearly knocked myself out. As I stood up and placed my hand on my head I could feel the blood oozing out of my hair and scalp. I was quite stunned and had it not been for a man who came to my assistance I could have been in serious trouble. He dragged me out of the water and got me some immediate medical attention but fortunately it was not a deep cut and I had only grazed my scalp.

Next morning, nursing a sore head, I had to say farewell to Keith Barclay and Flight Lieutenants Edwards and Brearley who had looked after me so well. During the short time that I had spent at Gaydon they had gone out of their way to make me feel welcome and teach me some of the basic principles of operations work. Although I did not know it at the time, I was destined to meet up with Keith again many years later, and also another member of the operations staff who I had not exactly got on with! Even though the RAF was a large organisation, it never ceased to amaze me how one met up with old friends time and time again in the most unusual circumstances.

CHAPTER 4

RAF Shawbury

The first thing I noticed as my taxi approached the RAF Shawbury (after an easy train journey via Birmingham and Shrewsbury) was that there were large numbers of aircraft such as Blackburn Beverleys and Avro Shackletons piled up on the perimeter. It looked like most of them had been there for some time; as they had all been cannibalised it was clear that they would never fly again. Some of the Beverleys had been on the strength of 34 Squadron that had been disbanded at Seletar Singapore in 1967. Then they had been flown into Shawbury to be disposed of by 27 Maintenance Unit, and they were a sorry sight as we approached the guard room.

RAF Shawbury has a long history dating back to the First World War when was been used by a number of training squadrons. Number 9 Training Depot Station was based there. 90 Squadron was the first proper unit to arrive in October 1917, but it failed to become operational before it moved in December that year. 131 Squadron arrived in March 1918, equipped with the FE2b and it remained at Shawbury until August. 137 Squadron arrived in April with the DH 9, but departed soon after. In 1918 the airfield was closed down.

RAF Shawbury was re-commissioned on 13 April 1938, and the first unit to be based there was 11 Service Flight Training School (SFTS), equipped with Hawker Harts and the Hawker Audax, the army co-operation version. By 1940, the units had re-equipped and it had sixty-six Air Speed Oxfords and twenty-two Fairey Battles on strength, along with forty Harts. Shawbury was never a front-line airfield and the nearest it got to fulfilling that role was when the Defiants or Hurricanes of 96 Squadron, based at nearby Cranage, landed there.

In 1942, 11 SFTS changed its title to become 11 (P) Advanced Flying Unit (AFU), with two satellite airfields at Wheaton and Perton. In January 1944, 11 (P) AFU moved out to another small grass airfield nearby called Calveley. There were a number of accidents involving the Airspeed Oxford, one of them involving the father of the director of The Royal Air Force Museum, Dr Fopp. In July 1944, Squadron Leader Fopp's Oxford, ED281, collided with another aircraft, ED399. The latter crashed to the ground killing all those on board while Squadron Leader Fopp managed to get his severely damaged aircraft on the ground, despite the fact it had lost its elevator on the port side and suffered other structural damage to the tail.

During February 1944, the Central Navigation School had moved to Shawbury, equipped with the Vickers Wellington Mk XIII, and in October that year it became the Empire Air Navigation School (EANS). By late 1945 it had been re-equipped with the Halifax, Lancaster and Mosquito, but it also had a single Mustang on charge as well for fighter navigation training. In February 1950, the EANS changed its name to the Central Navigation and Control School, and was then renamed again in early 1963 to become the Central Air Traffic Control School (CAATC).

When I arrived in September 1968, the school was still equipped with many of the same Vampires and the Hunting Percival Provost trainers it had flown in 1963. The piston-engined Provosts spent all their service life at Shawbury flying with the CAATC. They remained in service until 14 October 1969, when the final flight of twelve aircraft flew in formation over North Shropshire to mark the end of an era. The last airworthy example was WW937, kept in storage at Shawbury for two months before being flown to Halton on 30 October 1969. After being used for training for a number of years, it was bought by a private collector and allocated the civilian registration G-BKHP.

My first impression of the station was good, and I was very surprised to be allotted my own room in a smart new accommodation block with an excellent view of a distant wood. We were told later that the accommodation blocks had been modelled on college dormitories, and each room had its own study area, which included a desk and chair. The facilities that we had at Shawbury were a complete contrast to those I had experienced at Gaydon.

One thing that I could not fail to notice was the continuous noise of jet aircraft flying around in the circuit, often accompanied by the prattle of a piston engine. I soon discovered that the aircraft were De Havilland Vampires T 11s and piston-engined Provost T 1s that belonged to the CAATC. Both types were in the final years of their service with the RAF, and the Provost was a particularly rare aircraft, which had been replaced by the BAC Jet Provost. The Vampire, which had been replaced as a front-line aircraft by the Venom in the mid-1950s, was equally rare, and to see so many of them still flying was a privilege indeed. From morning until early evening the aircraft flew around the circuit allowing air traffic controllers under training to guide them and practice approaches and area radar work.

On the Friday morning we were introduced to our course tutor, Sergeant Williams, who gave us some preliminary notes on what our lectures would be about during the first week. Our tutor was a youngish looking man whose only blemish in his appearance was that his uniform appeared at least one size too big for him. The left breast pocket of his tunic displayed the General Service Medal, but he was a quiet man and obviously very knowledgeable on his subject. When he had formally introduced himself to some of my fellow students, he gave us the good news was that our course would not begin until the following week, which gave us the weekend to settle in.

Our course was the Assistant Air Traffic Controller's Course, Number 130. There were a total of eighteen students, including eight women, some of whom were very good looking. Among the airmen were a small number I had met on my basic training course at Swinderby, including Alan Kirkin, the cadet who had been awarded the Certificate of Merit at our passing out parade.

Over a period of seven weeks we were to have a total of forty-four lectures on the main air traffic control course, and another thirteen on a secondary signals course. The latter covered such subjects as radio communication, commuted aerial direction finding (ADF), basic radar principles, instrument landing systems, radio and radar aids to navigation aids.

Our first lecture on the Monday morning was about RAF policy and organisation, the administration of an RAF station, and how each wing was dependent upon one another. We were informed that air traffic control came under the control of Flying Wing, and under the command of the OC Flying, who held the rank of wing commander. Under him was the senior air traffic control officer, who held the rank of squadron leader and normally had his office in the control tower.

We were issued with a brown folder in which to keep our notes, with an index of what order the lectures were to be given. Lecture Number 1: Joint Military Civil Policy and Organisation; Number 2: Air Traffic Control Staff; Number 3: Liaison with other sections, as mentioned above; Number 4: the Classification of Aerodromes. This was one of the first really interesting

Course 130 at the Air Traffic Control Training School at RAF Shawbury in October 1968. I am standing in the middle row fourth from the right with my fringe hanging over my right eye! Although the length of hair at the back and sides was subject to regulations, that on top of the head was not, and I took full advantage. Our very tolerant Instructor, Sergeant Williams, is in the middle of the front row.

lectures because it actually dealt with matters concerning aviation rather than administration.

We learned about the different roles played by Master Diversion Airfields, Standard Aerodromes, Miscellaneous Aerodromes and Emergency Aerodromes. We were told that the most important of these was the Master Diversion Airfield because it was open 24 hours a day and continuously monitored VHF and UHF radio frequencies. Those included the emergency frequencies of 12.1.5 and 243 Mhz and the NATO common approach frequency of 122.1. By comparison, Miscellaneous Aerodromes were often little more than Relief Landing Grounds, and were the least important.

The lectures were given in a large spacious classroom in one of the many red-brick buildings on Shawbury's domestic site. Between normal lectures we were given a special study period but told in no uncertain fashion that the failure to pass the final examination with a pass rate of 70 per cent could mean that the airman or airwoman would be designated for general duties. They might only be offered another attempt to pass the exam or re-mustered to another trade if their assessments were above average. We all knew that the term General Duties (GD) was mockingly referred to as 'General Dog's Body', and none of us wanted to become one of those!

Discipline was nothing like that at Swinderby, and for some reason the SWO never bothered us. We still had to march around camp when we were going to lectures and there was an informal parade most mornings to check for haircuts and dress. We were naturally expected to be of a smart appearance; we were inspected just to ensure that we had a crease in our trousers and our hair was not on the collar.

One of the first practical things that we learned was the sending and receiving of signals using the Morse code. Sergeant Williams explained that within a week we would have to learn all twenty-six letters. Then we would be tested by having to identify ten letters that were to be flashed to us with an Aldis lamp. For days on end we practised, sitting in small groups, flashing the letters to one another. We drank, ate and slept the Morse code, and for the best part of a week it was the only topic of conversation in the NAAFI and in the bar.

Most of us began by learning how to send an SOS message, which was made up of three dots, three dashes and another three dots. Then gradually we picked up the rest of the code letter by letter until we knew each one instinctively. Finally, the day of the exam arrived, and with one exception, everyone got ten out of ten. The airman who failed would also fail many other aspects of the course and he was not destined to pass.

Some of the meteorological lectures, given by one of the senior meteorological officers at Shawbury, were very interesting and we learned how to differentiate between fog and mist and haze. Fog, we were told, only existed when the visibility was less than 1,000 yards. Mist only existed when visibility was 1,100 yards or more, and it was caused by the presence of water droplets in the air. When visibility was 1,100 yards or more and there were suspended solid particles in the air such as smoke, dust and sand, it was referred to as haze. Compared to the weathermen who were officially known as 'scientific officers', our understanding of the weather was quite basic, but it enlightened us a lot.

One of our practical exercises was to go outside and stand with our backs to the wind to understand the principles of Buys Ballot's Law, which dictates the connections between pressure and wind. The law states that if an observer in the northern hemisphere stands with his back to the wind, the area of low pressure is on the left. Therefore the wind will blow in an anti-clockwise direction around low pressure and in a clockwise direction around high pressure. The day we did this exercise there was hardly any wind at all, and there were many arguments about where the area of low pressure was.

RAF Shawbury was also used to train the Fleet Air Arm aircraft handlers, also known as matlows, in air traffic procedures; while we were there a large number of them arrived from HMS *Eagle*. We were warned well in advance that having been at sea for a long period of time, the sailors could be rather boisterous. It was claimed that they had a tendency to take over the camp and all the available women as well if they could get away with it. The first sign indicating that they had arrived were white cigarette packets lying on the ground, which displayed the symbol of an anchor. We knew the cigarettes were only issued on board Royal Navy vessels and sure enough, within a few hours, their presence was well and truly felt in the NAAFI.

The Fleet Air Arm was undergoing change, and in 1967, 890 Squadron had become the last unit to equip with the Sea Vixen before it was scheduled to re-equip with the new Rolls-Royce-powered Spey-engined Phantom F 4K. The *Eagle* was equipped with sea Vixens of 899 Squadron and Buccaneer S2s of 800 Squadron. Other carriers included HMS *Victorious* carrying Buccaneers, Sea Vixens and the Gannet AEW 3s. HMS *Hermes* was also equipped with Sea Vixens and Buccaneers. The Phantoms and Buccaneers were soon to be transferred to the RAF as the aircraft carrier was judged too expensive to maintain.

In September, while we were at Shawbury, it was announced that redundancies arising from the phasing out of carrier operations would be made in two stages. The first 750 sailors would be made redundant between October and December 1970, and the lion's share, a further 3,000, between January 1972 and March 1973. With all the cutbacks in manpower and equipment, the matlows may not have had much of a future in the navy to look forward to, but those at Shawbury still knew how to enjoy themselves.

We soon discovered that the matlows had actually arrived earlier that morning, but had gone straight to a local pub in Stanton. From previous visits, some of them had got to know the landlord well and had arranged with him to unofficially open the White Swan at dawn. Subsequently, by the time they turned up in the NAAFI, the matlows had spent most of the day in the pub and they were drunk and very noisy. Most of them were considerably older than the average RAF airmen on air traffic courses, and they were also far more experienced in the ways of the world. Within no time at all, they had rounded up most of the women to sit at their tables, and all we could do was to sit and watch with envy!

Some of the matlows, who we called 'fish heads', were quite friendly, and over the rest of the course we got to know them quite well. They were diverse in their skills and experience, but many of them were veterans of the Royal Navy and had served on HMS *Ark Royal* as well as HMS *Eagle*. For them, the course at Shawbury was a 'run ashore' and a bit of fun, but it was essential that they passed the air traffic course to get promoted.

It was while I was at Shawbury that I first heard the term 'penguins' being used to describe a certain type of officer on ground duties. At the time I did not understand what it meant, but later on someone explained that it was a derogatory term for a pilot (or other aircrew member) who had his wings, but could no longer fly. Quite often this was either because they had been medically downgraded, or were simply too old and not considered safe anymore. Many of the controllers who passed through Shawbury on radar courses were officers who could have been described as penguins, but because of their flying experience, they made good controllers. Our paths rarely crossed at Shawbury, but on the odd occasion that we bumped into them on the station, we threw them a hefty salute.

After Britain's withdrawal from Aden and other Gulf states, a large number of the RAF's redundant aircraft had been placed in long-term storage at Shawbury and most of them were still in excellent condition. There were Twin Pioneers, Beavers and Hawker Hunters, most of which had only recently returned from the Far East. The Twin Pioneers had previously been on the strength of 21 and 152 Squadrons that had been disbanded at the end of 1967 after returning from Aden and Bahrain respectively. A Comet C2, XK698, that had been withdrawn from service with 216 Squadron earlier in the year, was housed in one hangar. The aircraft that had originally held the civil registration G-AMXL was eventually broken up at St Athan in 1973.

We were also privileged to be shown around a Second World War fighter-bomber, Hawker Typhoon 1B MN 235, which was being prepared to be handed over to the RAF Museum at Hendon. It was being presented on behalf of the American Smithsonian Institute and 27 MU had been given the job of restoring it to its former glory. The handing over ceremony, which involved Dr John Tanner, the director of the RAF Museum, and Wing Commander Gifkin, the commanding officer of RAF Shawbury, took place on 19 November. By that time our course was complete and Shawbury was just a happy memory.

While we were at Shawbury, all airmen – but not airwomen (that was a sore point) – had to perform the role of 'duty airman'. This was a standard duty on most RAF stations, and the designated airman was responsible for closing down the NAAFI and other buildings like station headquarters, although the duty varied according to the station's demands. The duty airman reported to the guard room at 7 a.m. and worked under the command of the orderly sergeant and the orderly officer until 7 a.m. the following morning.

It was my bad luck that I was rostered in station routine orders to carry out the role of duty airman just after the Royal Navy had arrived, and I knew I would have trouble getting the matlows to leave the NAAFI. Sure enough, by 9 p.m. that night, as they had done every other weekday night, the matlows gathered all their tables together. Two separate groups were in the process of piling up beer tins to see which one of them could get closest to the ceiling before they collapsed. Many of the cans fell on the floor and the place was in uproar with beer spilling out onto the tables and carpets. Although as the duty airman, I was not directly responsible for what happened, I did have a responsibility to maintain some kind of order, but when I asked them to stop I was totally ignored.

The keys for the NAAFI had to be returned to the guard room by 11.30 p.m., but by that time the matlows were still drinking and refusing to be moved. There was no alterative but for me to report to the guard room and request the help of the duty sergeant. In the guard room an RAF policeman said he would help me to deal with it, and told me not to bother the duty sergeant. The policeman ordered me back to the NAAFI to tell those who still had drinks to leave immediately otherwise the RAF police would be dealing with them. As I walked out of the door he shouted and said, 'Oh, and tell them there's a Shore Patrol on the way from Turnhill! I'll give them a ring now.'

I did as I was ordered; walking back into the NAAFI, I called for silence, and amid heckling and cat-calls, I broke the news. Not all those present were matlows, and despite the fact that they were wearing civvies, I knew some of them to be RAF trainees from the senior course. They were quite dismissive of my authority and insulted me, with some shouting 'Get yer knees brown'. However, their abuse was cut short when the doors suddenly swung open behind me and two RAF policemen, a sergeant and the corporal from the guard room, marched in, accompanied by a young flight lieutenant who was the orderly officer.

It suddenly went very quiet; it was the orderly officer who broke the silence by making references to the fact that members of the senior service did not know how to behave themselves. He reminded them that they were guests on an RAF station and they were expected to behave accordingly.

Apparently there had been trouble at a local pub involving some other matlows and he said that measures needed to be taken to prevent any further outbreaks of ill-discipline. The corporal went around the room taking their names, ranks and numbers and I finally got to close the NAAFI at about midnight. I had a few hours sleep in a bunk in the guard room, and I was very happy to finish my stint at 7 a.m. the next morning.

Like many other trades and professions, air traffic control is as much about the language as anything else. There are ETAs – Estimated Time of Arrival – and ATAs – Actual Time of Arrival. Then there is the 'Q' code, which is an important element of air traffic language that some students struggled to learn. There is the QFE, the pressure setting that the pilot sets on his altimeter on the ground before take-off, or as he approaches an airfield to land. The QFE represents the aerodrome level pressure and is given in milibars, although the Americans use inches as a measurement instead. The QNH is the mean sea level pressure, adjusted by ICAO standards, to an aerodrome's height above sea level. A pilot sets it on the altimeter when he leaves the vicinity of the circuit. Basically, the QNH is the same as the QFE, but adjusted to the height that a particular airfield is above sea level. One milibar of pressure is equal to approximately 30 feet, and so if an airfield is 60 feet above sea level, the QNH will be approximately two milbars greater than the QFE. It could get quite complicated, especially if one had no previous experience, but fortunately I had learned all about it during my aircraft spotting days. There were many other elements of the Q code, QDM – a magnetic bearing, QTE – a true bearing, QSY – change frequency.

Not only does air traffic control have its own language, but it also has its own time zone; all the times written on flight plans are given in what is referred to as 'Zulu Time'. It is based on Greenwich Mean Time, and it ensures that wherever an aircraft is in the world, its pilot and crew are working on the same standard time as everyone else. Local time is referred to as 'Alpha Time', and although it may sometimes be used for details of local flights, it would never be accepted on a flight plan.

We had all heard about the 'Mayday' call and the international distress signal 'SOS', but none of us realised that there were three different states of emergency that could be declared. Mayday was the highest state of emergency and meant that an aircraft and its crew were in serious or imminent danger. The second state of a distress call had the radio prefix 'Pan', meaning a pilot was in need of assistance but might be able to overcome the his difficulties. It was typically used if a pilot was lost or if he was running short of fuel; its W/T prefix was 'XXX'. The lowest state of emergency was a 'Safety' call that had the R/T prefix of 'Securite', and W/T prefix 'TTT'. The safety call was soon to be phased out, and so we were subsequently told to forget about it!

After Sergeant Williams had given us lecture 27 on R/T procedures, we were taken to one of the classrooms that had been turned into a simulated radio room. Sergeant Williams sat at the back of a room in a cubicle, calling each student up on the R/T, requesting information. The R/T was actually an intercom system.

The student going through the exercise had to gather details about the 'aircraft', such as whether it was an Andover from Devon or a Devon from Andover (irrespective of the fact that Andover had closed many years before). In turn, the student would provide information for the 'pilot' (Sergeant Williams) about the weather and airfield serviceability at a specified airfield. We were instructed not to gabble on the R/T, to make sure that we got the pitch, tone and rhythm of our speech correct, and to avoid using 'er' at all cost. Personal greetings were frowned upon and students were not allowed to eat or smoke in the simulator.

To help them find such information, students were given Flight Information Publications (FLIPS) that held the details of all RAF and civilian airfields in Britain. They contained the runway headings of all RAF stations, the frequencies in use, the LCN (Load Classification Number), which gave an indication of what size of aircraft the runways could accept, and the airfields' hours of operation. There was a similar book for European airfields and in theory the flight information trainee had everything he needed at his finger tips – he just had to learn how to find it. Sometimes it fell to us students to play the role of the pilot in the simulator, and we would ask questions like, 'On what airway is Deans Cross located?' or 'Request a frequency to call Preston Airways in order to join Airway Blue 1 at Ottringham.'

Most of the questions seemed a bit tame and so I began to have a bit of fun, and against all the rules, I would call up and pretend to be a civilian airliner in difficulties. In an American drawl I would call, 'Mayday, Mayday, this Clipper 1, en-route New York to Frankfurt. We are a Boeing 707 with two engines on fire request immediate assistance.' In most cases the sound quality in the simulator was so poor that those playing the flight information assistant could not distinguish one voice from another. They were encouraged to take every call seriously and be as helpful as they could, but sometimes it could be difficult, especially when I was in the control room!

All RAF aircraft have their own call signs; we had to become familiar with the more common ones like 'RAF AIR' and 'ASCOT'. The latter was short for 'Air Support Command Operational Training' and often used by the crews flying the VC10 and Hercules on operational and training flights. There were are also special call signs to indicate that a member of the royal family was on board an aircraft, the main one being 'Kitty Hawk' to indicate it was carrying the Queen. Prince Phillip had his own call sign and when he was at the controls he used 'Rainbow'. The royal family was even allocated its own airspace that was referred to as 'Purple Airspace'; it seemed they could even dictate the colour of the sky!

We also had to learn and identify the 'speechless procedure' that was only ever used when a pilot lost the use of his VHF or UHF radio. Normally in such cases, the carrier wave still functioned and it could be used to make a distinct 'clicking' sound. The controller would ask questions on the same frequency that the suspected clicking was heard, and his first task would be to identify the aircraft. He might ask for instance, 'Can you confirm that your call sign is Mike Bravo Delta 35?' One click meant 'yes', two clicks 'no', and three clicks 'say again'. As we had already learned, four clicks in the Morse code spelt the letter 'H' and when that was transmitted it meant that the pilot was requesting a homing signal.

There is an old saying, 'a little knowledge is a dangerous thing', and in my case it turned out to be correct! As previously mentioned, for at least three years before joining the RAF I had spent most of my spare time on the terraces at Manchester Airport aircraft spotting. I had a Shorrocks Mk VI VHF band radio, and from listening to that I knew quite a lot about the language of aviation and the procedures that were used by air traffic controllers. A lot of that knowledge on frequencies, airways clearances and the phonetic language had held me in good stead. What I had not taken into account was that military aviation is a different beast entirely.

One evening, I bumped into Sergeant Williams down at the Elephant and Castle public house. He liked his tipple, but he was surprised to see me at the bar so early in the evening, drinking with one or two of the locals. After getting over the initial shock, we sat down at a table together and he very kindly pointed out that my time would be much better spent going through the notes on the day's lectures and revising in my room. Sergeant Williams said he knew that I had some experience of what the course covered, but that I should build on my knowledge rather than take it for granted. He also reminded me that I had barely achieved a pass mark on my most recent progress test, and it was not good enough. I knew he was right and I promised him that I would change my ways, before it was too late and I would be forced into to changing my trade!

As we approached the end of our course, Sergeant Williams took us on a guided tour of the airfield that included a visit to the control tower. Except for my short-lived experience at Gaydon, it was the first time that I had a look around an RAF tower. We were split into two parties, and my group was first taken into the approach room. The room was blacked out and at first it was difficult to see exactly what was going on, but eventually the shadowy figures sitting at the consoles became clearer.

We were instructed on how the new mini-com system worked. Compared to the hand-held radios that we had been using in training, it seemed so modern and easy to use. The mini-com panel was a small unit of neat switches and each switch controlled a single frequency, such as those used for the approach and local control. Pushed forward it engaged the frequency in both transmission and receiver modes, but in the middle position it only monitored the frequency and one could not transmit. With the switch pulled back, the frequency was effectively turned off.

There were a number of radar consoles where controllers were sitting with headphones on, talking to pilots of the aircraft that were practising approaches. Down at the end of the room was the Precision Approach Radar (PAR) that was used to talk down pilots when the visibility was bad. It consisted of two screens, one on top of the other, which displayed the extended centre line of the runway and the elevation of the 3-degree glide path. That meant that if pilots were on the correct glide scope, the aircraft descended on the approach at 300 feet per mile. We stood just a few feet behind the controller in silence, and watched as he talked down a Vampire pilot; it was a very interesting experience. Even though it was only a practice PAR approach, the controller seemed very assured and we learned that confidence was a vital part of being a good controller. A pilot placed his life and that of his crew in the hands of the controller, and to make it work he had to have faith in him and obey every command. When a pilot deferred his authority to a controller, he wanted someone who he could rely on; giving instructions in a clear calm voice was vital to the procedure.

From the blacked-out approach room, we made our way up to local control, which was bathed in sunshine. The controller and his assistant sat on a raised platform, with the controller on the left and his assistant on his right. There was a lot of activity, and it was important for us not to distract the controller who was talking to a number of pilots that were flying in the circuit. The frequency he was using was on the ultra high frequency band.

It was called 'Local Control', and it was the same facility as on a civil airfield that used Very High Frequency radio and was called Tower.

We had a wonderful all-round view of the airfield, and being situated close to the runway, we got a good close up view of the Vampires and Provost as they approached, some to land but others to overshoot. We were introduced to the 'Crash Phone', a large red plastic telephone that sat on the top of the console on the controller's left. After a quick call to the medical centre and the fire section to warn them, Sergeant William picked up the phone and it immediately lit up red and made a strange warbling noise. He explained that it was only to be used to alert the fire section and medical centre on the occasions such as a crash or other major incident on or off the airfield.

Next we were shown the lighting panel, which was a large grey metal box in the corner of the room that controlled all the airfield lighting. With so many aircraft in the circuit, Sergeant Williams was careful not to interfere with any of the major lighting systems, such as the 5 Bar Approach Lighting or the Visual Approach Slope Indicators (VASI). The latter was a ground aid that consisted of two banks of lights that were situated close to the runway threshold. If a pilot was on the correct glide path then the lights at the front glowed white, while those behind them glowed red. If he was too high, both sets appeared white, and if he was too low then they glowed red for danger. Our sergeant demonstrated how to 'pulse' the lights on and off, and explained the workings of what looked like a very complicated system.

The local controller's assistant, a young leading aircraftsman, who himself had only recently passed out at Shawbury, told us all about his duties. He said his main role was to keep the log book and note the take-off times and landing times of all aircraft, and in between that to keep the controller happy with a regular supply of tea and coffee! It was a pleasant tour around the tower and as we descended the stairs to leave, it was hard to believe that very shortly we would all be performing similar duties to those we had just witnessed.

As we approached our final examination, we all had to fill in a form to declare what station or part of the country we would like to be posted to on completion of the course. It was claimed that the clerks at the records section at Innsworth had a perverse sense of humour, and if an airman applied to be posted to the south coast, he probably stood a good chance of being sent to Scotland. However, we were assured that our request would be met wherever possible, and I put down my first choice as Heathrow Radar, where my old fiend Bob Bailey was still stationed. I put my second choice down as Preston, where the RAF had small number of staff at the air traffic control centre at Barton Hall. That was 200 miles further north, but it was also quite close to my home in Manchester.

The examination was held on a Monday morning, which was not a good time after a pleasant, alcohol-fuelled weekend. Everyone was very nervous, even the couple of swats on the course, but Sergeant Williams pointed out that we did not have to rack our brains searching for the answers, because they were already there on the examination papers; it was a multiple-choice examination, and all we had to do was tick the right boxes. There were possible four answers to every question, and as one of them was clearly a decoy anyway in most instances, it usually came down to the best of three. The down side was that the pass mark was 70 per cent, and anything below that was a clear failure.

The examination went reasonably well, and as usual on these occasions, when it was over everyone congregated in the NAAFI to compare notes. During the afternoon, Sergeant Williams took us around on a final tour of the airfield. The highlight was a look around the Comet XK698. In small groups we were taken up to the flight deck, and a former pilot explained the layout of the instruments and controls. It was a great afternoon, but everyone felt quite tense. We did not get our results until the following morning.

With the exception of a single airman, everyone passed; for the lad who had failed, there was great sympathy. He disappeared soon after the results were posted, and no doubt he did not want to be embarrassed for letting the course down. We heard that he had already been classed as a Trade Assistant General, and posted out straight away. He might eventually have been given another opportunity to learn a trade, but first he would have to have undergone further strict assessments.

The rest of us were now promoted to the rank of Leading Aircraftsman (and Leading Aircraftwomen), and were issued with our badges of rank that had to be sown on the sleeves of our best blue uniforms immediately. Not very many of us were competent with a needle and thread, so most of the girls volunteered to sow them on for us. Some girls charged a small fee for their services while others just settled for a drink at the bar, but it was well worth it for their nimble finger work.

Just a few hours after we had received out results, our postings were listed on the main notice board. Everyone scrambled around, eager to learn where they would be spending the next few years; while some were disappointed, others were happy that they had got what they had applied for. Beside my name was written 'RAF Manston', and I was not sure whether to feel happy or disappointed because I did not know where it was. Sergeant William told me that it was a Master Diversion Airfield in Kent, but I was still none the wiser! For the time being I put my posting out of my mind, and after we collected our travel warrants from the general office, it was time to celebrate!

Our celebration party was held in the White Swan in Stanton, the Scrumpy pub popular with the Fleet Air Arm. It was Bonfire Night and the locals had built a large fire at the back of the pub and put on special goods such as treacle and toffee apples. I got lucky with a girl I'd had my eye on for a while, and because I managed to get one of the best seats in the house in front of the pub's roaring fire, she came to sit on my lap. She was a WAAF who had arrived on a recent intake. Such was the competition to get both a comfortable seat and the company of a good-looking female, that I paid various people to go to the bar and get our drinks.

The only person who I trusted was Sergeant Williams, who looked after my seat and my WAAF while I went to the toilet. When I returned he tried to pull rank on me, but then reluctantly got up and with a smile bought another round of drinks. Paddy, who had failed his examination, was present for some of the time, but he disappeared again at some point during the evening – it can't have been much fun for him. At the end of the night, RAF transport arrived to take us back to Shawbury and there were many drunken hugs, kisses and handshakes.

The following morning we went through the emotional turmoil again as we waited by the guard room for the bus to take some of us to Cosford Station. There were more handshakes and farewell kisses before we boarded the bus, and the last thing I remember seeing as we drove past the guard room was Paddy cleaning the windows outside. It was a sombre sight, and reminded me of the fate of those who failed to pass their trade examinations.

At Euston Station it was time to say the final good-bye to my final two companions. While they headed to Paddington and the south-west, I headed for Victoria Station and the south-east. At Victoria I caught the train bound for Ramsgate. There were twelve carriages and I was told that only the front eight coaches went to Ramsgate, which caused me quite a bit of confusion. As the train rumbled out past the power station and across Battersea Bridge, I realised that I was heading towards a new life and a new culture!

CHAPTER 5

RAF Manston

I arrived at Manston during the late afternoon of 6 November 1968. I felt very tired and hungry as I had been on the move since early that morning and completed two long train journeys. Shawbury now seemed no more than a distant memory, and I felt quite anxious about what I should find at Manston, whether I would meet another belligerent station warrant officer or RAF policeman. However, when the taxi dropped me off outside a wooden hut that passed for the guard room, I discovered that there were no RAF police, and the station was manned by the MoD police, who were effectively civilians.

The duty policeman that afternoon was Tom, a robust and friendly officer who offered me a nice hot cup of tea straight away. He told me that the airmen's mess would be closing soon, but that first I should go to the bedding store or I would not get any sheets or blankets issued. Also, only the duty store man or the SWO could allocate me a room in one of the accommodation blocks, so I had to report there as soon as possible.

With a little difficulty I found the bedding store and met the store man who was just closing up for the day. He seemed quite flustered by my arrival because he had not been told that anyone was being posted in; the SWO had already gone home. The store man told me that the heating had broken down in the accommodation block and he was under strict instructions from the SWO not to issue any keys for rooms until it was repaired. The only place that I could stay was in the annexe, which he me informed me was the long wooden building behind the sergeants' mess. Unfortunately, he forgot to mention that the annexe was already full of airmen from Waddington, who were servicing a couple of Vulcan bombers that were taking part in a 'Tacky Val' (Micky Finn Tactical Evaluation) exercise.

Staggering under the weight of my RAF-issue holdall and bedding, I made my way around the back to the annexe and to my surprise it looked remarkably similar to the hut that I had stayed in at Gaydon. When I got to the door I found that the doorway was blocked by an airman who was on his hands and knees, polishing the corridor. He was totally absorbed in what he was doing, dipping a yellow duster into a large tin of Mansion House and applying it to the lino.

He totally ignored the fact that I was trying to get past, so I tried to step over him by lifting my bags into the air, but then disaster struck! While I was squeezing past, my holdall fell out of my hand and hit a fire extinguisher that was sitting on a small white box next to a bucket of sand. White foam exploded from the nozzle as the extinguisher hit the ground, and within seconds I was covered in it, as was most of the corridor and the airman who had been polishing it.

I soon discovered that the airman polishing the corridor was in fact a corporal, and the expletives that he shouted at me as he tried to get out of the way of the foam are not fit for print! He told me that he was polishing the corridor for the CO's Inspection the following morning, and I would have clear up the mess and make good the damage. However, before I could do anything I had to find a room and tidy myself up, but that also proved a difficult task. Nearly every room was occupied, and the few that were empty had no lockers or mattresses. In the end I found an empty room that was only unoccupied because it was full of litter; I dragged a bed from another room, then I dumped my sheets and blankets and reported to the corporal to begin clearing up the mess and start re-polishing the corridor.

By the time I had finished I was exhausted, and after getting approval from the grumpy corporal, I made my way across to the airmen's mess, only to find it had closed over an hour earlier. Someone suggested that I try the NAAFI next door, but that was also closed. I enquired at the guard room and Tom, the same friendly policeman I had met before, told me that a bus for Margate would be leaving in about fifteen minutes.

I ran back to my room and quickly changed out of my sodden best blue uniform and into some civvies. As I stood by the guard room, I nearly missed the bus because I didn't recognise it; I was used to buses being big red or green double-deckers, like those in Manchester. This was a small AEC Regent single-decker of the East Kent Bus Company and it looked more like a coach than a bus. As I was the only person at the bus stop, I had to jump out in front of it to get the driver to pull over. Life in the south was going to take some getting used to!

Margate on a bleak winter's night was dead! However, I found a fish and chip shop by the memorial on the seafront, and after scoffing them down I went in search of a good pub. I ended up in the Pilot Boat, a relatively new public house on the seafront near the railway station. There was hardly anyone in the place except a young couple who were sitting on their own in the corner canoodling with each other. They kept the juke box going on repeat playing 'I Heard It Through The Grape Vine' by Marvin Gaye. After the first couple of plays I began to feel quite depressed, but after another six or seven times I felt positively suicidal. I had a yearning to be back home in Manchester, and that feeling was made more intense when the barmaid told me she was from Stockport.

Unable to stand the delights of the town any more, I decided to head back to Manston, but I soon discovered that the last bus had left a long time ago. I went to inquire about getting a taxi, but by now I had only had a few pounds to last me until I got paid again, and the fare would have taken a large portion of it. Because the journey on the bus had only taken seven or eight minutes, I made a rash decision and decided to walk back to Manston. I found my way out of town down Belgrave Road and along Tivoli Road, but further on, by the outskirts by the cemetery, the street lighting ended abruptly and the night was suddenly very dark indeed. Although I have never been afraid of the dark, I suddenly felt quite anxious as there was no sign of the airfield that I had presumed was just a short distance up the road.

As I passed by the cemetery I broke into a trot, and the only noise came from some overhead power lines that were arcing and making a loud buzzing noise. Soon I became very tired and realised that it was a lot further than I had thought. Then I saw some headlights approaching in the distance, heading in my direction; I slowed down to let the driver see me and not run me over.

When it got closer, I turned around to see it was a police car, and as he slowly drove past me the officer motioned with his hand for me to approach him. He seemed quite suspicious at first, and he said he was looking for someone who had been involved in a fight in a pub in Margate. He asked me my name and when I showed him my RAF Identification Card his attitude change. Having checked my I.D., he offered me a lift; the warmth and comfort of the Hillman Imp was a welcome break from the dark damp air outside.

The policeman dropped me off at the guard room and went in for a cup of tea, while I made my way back to the squalid conditions I had left several hours before. I was so tired that I just threw a couple of blankets on the bed and tried to go to sleep, which I eventually did, but in the early hours of the morning I woke up to the worst tooth ache I have ever had. I had no Asprin, Anadin or any other pain killers with me, and I had to wait until 8 a.m. for the medical centre to open. The sergeant duty medic told me that Manston did not have a resident dentist and that I would have to travel to Ramsgate to see a civilian dentist later that morning. Within the hour I was on an East Kent bus again, travelling down to Ramsgate Harbour.

As the bus drove across the airfield I saw an interesting collection of aircraft that belonged to Manston's resident Invicta Airlines. There were a couple of old DC 4s sitting on the apron, but waiting for the scrap man's torch were a number of Vickers Vikings that had recently been taken out of service.

As I passed through Manston village, I saw the local pub, the Jolly Farmer, for the first time; it had been the scene of much revelry by fighter pilots during Second World War. It was later to become one of my favourite

A good view of RAF Manston as a flight of Bristol Fighters from 2 Squadron fly over in May 1927.

watering holes, but at that moment I was in more urgent need of a dentist than a pub as I was still in agony!

After getting off the bus by the harbour, I made my way up to Nelson Crescent as instructed, and found the dentist without any trouble. He was a friendly enough sort, and although he introduced himself by his first name Tim, he behaved in a very professional manner. After a brief inspection of my teeth he told me that I had an abscess behind a molar and to get to it he would first have to remove the tooth, but that would be too painful to do immediately. What he recommended was that he give me an injection to help to relive the pain, then extract the tooth a in a few days' time when the swelling had gone down.

I accepted what he said and after the injection the pain receded almost immediately, so I travelled back to Manston on the bus and prepared to report to the control tower. I changed back into my best blue uniform and for the first time I noticed how badly stained it was after my encounter with the fire extinguisher the previous evening. It was in a terrible state, but my working blue uniform that lay at the bottom of my holdall was in an equally bad condition and I had no choice but to wear my best uniform.

As I approached the control tower it struck me for the first time just how far away it was from the main runway. The whitewashed building looked stranded in a position a quarter of a mile or so from where an aircraft was taking-off. On other stations that I had visited like Gaydon and Shawbury the control towers were situated in a central position close to the main runway, but Manston's tower seemed totally out of place. I was later to learn that a new control tower had been built as part of the fire section building that was positioned close to the main runway. For some strange reason, probably political or financial, it had been decided that it should not be used by air traffic control, and was used instead by the fire section as their watch office.

Approaching the administration office I felt rather nervous. I knocked on the door and introduced myself to a corporal, who in the dim light of the office stood staring at my stained tunic and trousers. He told me his name was Corporal Abbott and as he tutted away he asked me if I had a working blue uniform that I could wear. I told him that I did, but that I had not sown my LAC badges onto it and anyway, it also needed cleaning as it was crumpled up at the bottom of my holdall. Considering the circumstances, Corporal Abbott was very polite and took me up two short flights of stairs to the next level where the movements room was situated.

The control tower at Manston was unique because it was positioned nearly a quarter of a mile from the main runway. It was originally built by the side of the grass runway 24/06, and when the permanent new runway was opened in 1944 the control tower wasn't moved. The letters 'MN' in the Signal's Square in this aerial view indicate 'Manston'. The two windows on the top left were in the SATCO's office, and the white wall without any windows was the Radar Control Room. The air traffic Land Rover, call-sign 'Rover 1', can be seen parked up on the right.

On most other RAF stations it would have been called an air operations centre, but probably because Manston did not have a resident unit other than an Air Experience Flight it was known as 'Movements'. The corporal introduced me to the shift that was on duty, and then told me I would have to have an arrival interview with the Senior Air Traffic Controller (SATCO), Squadron Leader John Herrington. His office was in a room at the side of the approach room and Corporal Abbott knocked on the door and disappeared inside. A minute later he was out again and he gestured for me to follow him into the office.

Outside the office, Corporal Abbott told me to put my hat on, walk in to the office, stop in front of the SATCO, then salute and wait for him to speak. This all seemed very formal and as I marched in, memories of pay parades at Swinderby went through my mind. As I stood in front of the SATCO, he just stared at me as though I had suddenly sprouted another head or something. He mumbled, 'Good God, corporal, has this airman ... Bamford ... come straight from training?'

'Shawbury, sir,' I interjected, 'just passed out.' The SATCO looked puzzled.

'I've never seen anything like it,' he said. 'It's incredible! I am amazed you were allowed to get away with wearing that!!!' At that moment he pointed to my tunic to emphasise his point.

'It only happened last night, sir! I accidentally knocked over a fire extinguisher.' My admission seemed to make things worse; he turned his back on me and said to Corporal Abbott, 'Get this airman out of my office and see to it that he gets his uniform dry cleaned immediately. Then I will talk to him again!'

I was ordered to attention, saluted and marched out of the office in shame. Corporal Abbott was embarrassed by the SATCO's outburst, but some airmen who had overheard the proceedings were quite amused and had a good laugh at my expense. SAC Jim Burns, a Glaswegian, made light of the incident and offered me the loan of his tunic if I needed to go back into the SATCO's office again. The fact that he was a lot bigger than me made his offer all the more amusing and when, at his insistence, I put his tunic on, my arms disappeared up the sleeves. I decided to decline his generous offer!

It had been interesting 24 hours in which I had set off a fire extinguisher, ruined my best blue uniform, experienced the most excruciating toothache and upset the SATCO. First impressions cannot be made twice, and I had certainly got off to a bad start at Manston! The only good thing was that I learned that some of the people I would be working with liked a laugh and had a good sense of humour. It was just as well because I think my arrival had caused a lot of amusement and I had been the star turn.

When Corporal Abbot checked the shift roster, he told me that I was going to work on 'A' shift under Corporal Turner and Corporal 'Robbie' Roberts. They were on duty that afternoon, but the corporal said that I would be better working on days until the following week. He told me to report back to the tower the next morning, but before I went he explained the shift system. There were four 'watches', A, B, C and D. Each shift worked an afternoon from 12.20 a.m. until 5 p.m. and then the same watch worked the following morning from 8 a.m. until 12.20 a.m. After resting in the afternoon, it went on duty again from 5 p.m. until 8 a.m. the following morning. It was a long 15-hour shift, but after that we got two-and-a-half days off, in which we could be called upon for other duties.

After being shown around the tower and having everything explained to me, I visited the bedding store and asked when I was going to be able to move out of the old wooden hut and into a permanent room. Unfortunately, I bumped into the SWO, Flight Sergeant Brian Goddard. Almost on cue he told me to get my hair cut and to smarten myself up, but rather surprisingly he made no specific comments about the state of my uniform. The SWO told me I could not move into the main accommodation block until the heating was restored and that might be in a few weeks' time. It was a very daunting prospect for me to have to remain living in the wooden hut for that long, and deeply depressing!

That night I discovered that the NAAFI had just reopened, and although the place was quite empty, I got talking to an Irishman who I had bumped into a few times. He worked in the communications centre and introduced himself as 'Paddy'; he certainly had plenty of Irish charm and the gift of the gab. Over a few pints he told me that the room next to his was empty and that he had the key for it. The deal was sealed over another couple of pints of Guinness and by the end of the night I had moved my stuff to the room on the first floor.

At a time when most accommodation on other RAF stations consisted of four-man rooms, Manston was among a small number of stations that had single rooms. The large white painted 'H' Block had probably been built during the 1920s when 3 School of Technical Training was based there. It had rooms on two floors with access through either a door on the ground floor or up the wooden stairs to the first floor. Some rooms on one corridor were allocated as the overflow for the Sergeant's Mess, which was next door, and those rooms had sinks in them. Mine did not, but is was a comfortable room all the same, with a bed, small locker, tall locker, and a small table.

The next morning when I reported to the control tower I had a message to ring the SWO before 8.30 a.m. There was no indication of what it was about, but I thought that he might be checking up that I'd had my haircut or whether I'd moved into the main accommodation block without his permission. I began to prepare my excuses, but it was nothing to do with either haircuts or accommodation; he informed me that I had been put on general duties with another airman, Senior Aircraftsman Pete Abel.

Because I was the new boy, I had been nominated by air traffic control to act as a coalman for a few days. The SWO said that the two regular civilians had reported sick, but coal still needed to be delivered around the camp, and

An aerial reconnaissance photograph of RAF Manston taken by the Luftwaffe in 1940, when it was only a grass airfield. The landing ground is under the word 'Rollfeld' (runway) and the domestic site and buildings of the old School of Technical Training are at the top of the picture.

especially to married quarters. Someone had to do the job. I later learned that while I had been chosen because I was the new boy, Pete Abel was probably chosen because he often spoke his mind and had a reputation for being something of a 'bad boy'.

Within a matter of hours I discovered that my body had not been made for such strenuous work as humping bags of coal around. Since joining the RAF some five months earlier, I had put on some weight, but my humble frame was of a very light build and I still weighed only just over eight stone. However, for two days Pete and I struggled to load the coal into sacks from the chute in the coal yard on the Birchington Road, before loading them onto the lorry and delivering them around the station. Pete drove the old Komma wagon and I had to listen to him as he cursed and questioned the parentage of the SWO, the CO and the air traffic admin personnel in his own amusing way!

I found out that Pete was on the same watch that I had been assigned to, and although he complained a lot about everybody and everything, his cheery broad cockney humour always shone through. He had been in the RAF a long time, and I heard later that he had previously held the rank of corporal, but that had been demoted after committing a certain misdemeanour.

When we were stood down from our labour at the end of the second day, the SWO said that we were only being let off the duty early because we were needed to work that night in the control tower. Pete went absolutely berserk, and immediately rang the admin office to speak to Sergeant Sheldrake. The conversation was full of expletives and Pete told him that having worked all day he did not intend to work all night as well. The sergeant caved in and we were both released from our labouring duties, and stood down until the next shift began. The few days off gave me time to sort myself out, unpack and get my uniforms dry cleaned. My working blue uniform did not have even the shadow of a crease left, but after humping sacks of coal around in it, it was covered in dirt and coal dust.

During this period I got to know a few of the lads who lived on my corridor, and I saw Paddy again for the first time since we had met in the NAAFI a few nights before. I got to know him quite well and he became my first real friend on the station. He held the rank of senior aircraftsman, and worked in the communications centre on the second floor of the control tower. Paddy came from the Creggan Estate in Londonderry and was very aware of the troubles in Northern Ireland; he held strong political views that were not particularly in tune with those of the establishment! Working in such a sensitive environment as the communications centre, some people openly questioned how Paddy had got security clearance, but that was not my concern!

CHAPTER 6

Manston Control Tower

My first shift in air traffic at Manston began on 11 November when I was assigned to 'A' Watch and given the duties of the approach controller's assistant. That was probably because it was the easiest of the three main positions to learn; the job mainly involved sitting at a desk in the blacked out approach room, waiting for the telephone to ring, usually from someone requesting information about Manston's weather. At least once an hour we received telephone calls from Uxbridge, Wattisham and Thorney Island, checking the Manston weather and airfield serviceability.

Also, every hour on the hour the weather information had to be updated on the two perspex boards at each end of the room, in red chinagraph pencil. The most important information was the pressure settings, the QFE and the QNH, which were vital for aircraft safety. Manston was only 178 feet above sea level, and as one millibar of pressure is equal approximately to 30 feet, it meant that there should always be approximately 5-6 millibars difference between the two pressures. That was a good way to cross check them. It was a boring task and one had to be at the beck and call of the approach controllers, of which there were normally three on duty during the day.

There was the air traffic controller officer (ATCO) in charge of the shift, who normally held the rank of flight lieutenant, and a second controller who helped him to work the approach frequencies who was often referred to as the director. The third member of the shift was a specialist 'talk down' controller, and he worked on the Ground Controlled Approach (GCA) Radar. His job was to advise pilots on their aircraft's height (elevation), position in relation to the centre line (azimuth), and distance to run as they came in to land. This was a specialist task and a very skilled job, normally carried out by only the most experienced controllers whose advice was mandatory.

Any new movements that we received were written on the Movements Board, another large piece of perspex that was situated on the back wall directly in front of the radar screens, positioned so that the controller only had to look up to get information. The board had to be kept up to date with landing and take-off times recorded, and outbound movements deleted when they had finally cleared the airfield. When dealing with assistants at other airfields and stations, we had to ask for their initials in case there was a misunderstanding or wrong information was passed. We also had to give our initials for the same reason, and by the end of a shift you knew the person on the end of the telephone quite well!

In total contrast to the dark gloomy confines of the approach room, upstairs, local control was full of natural light, and with its panoramic view of the airfield it always felt like a good place to be. Immediately in front of us, looking towards the runway to the south-west, one could see the Swingate Masts, 22 miles away on the outskirts of Dover. They were sited on a piece of ground close to Dover Castle that had been an airfield during the First World War, from where the first squadrons of the Royal Flying Corps had departed for France in August 1914. Behind the controller's consol, over to the north, we could sometimes see Southend Pier, many miles away across the Thames Estuary.

At night the most prominent feature on the airfield was the large red Pundit light that sat behind the fire section, near the central taxiway. Most civil airports had green Pundit lights to identify them, but all military airfields and bases had red ones. The Manston beacon repeatedly flashed the letters 'MN' in Morse code (dash dash – dash dot) and it could be seen many miles away in Pegwell Bay and around the coast.

On a typical shift there were normally two airmen on duty in local control, the local controller was normally a senior NCO and his assistant was normally a senior aircraftsman. If the assistant did not get on with the controller, it could make for a long awkward shift, but most of the controllers were happy to chat, especially when it was quiet. Flight Sergeant Bob Kaye and Master Pilot Vic Brown were regular local controllers and they could be very amusing when they chose to be.

The assistant rarely got to speak over the R/T local control VHF frequency, and his main duty was to log the movements of all landings and take-offs. He was also responsible for communicating over the telephone

An unknown airman posing beside Manston's Radio Homing Beacon in the 1950s.

and squawk box about all aircraft movements with the Aircraft Servicing Flight (ASF) or Invicta Airways operations staff if it was a civil movement. His duty was to give them a ten-minute warning of any arrivals and inform Customs if the aircraft was arriving from a foreign destination.

The Pye radio set was also normally controlled by the assistant, and he maintained radio contact with all vehicles that were allowed out on to the airfield. There was a special log book in local control and all civilians going out on to the airfield had to sign in the book. If they did not have a Pye radio, then they would be accompanied by a service vehicle. Every RAF section had its own call sign and the air traffic Land Rover was called 'Rover 1'. The ASF Land Rover was 'ASF 1', the crash fire section Land

Rover was 'Crash 1', and the ambulance from the medical centre (known as the meat wagon) was 'Red Cross 1'.

The CO's call sign was 'Sunray', and we were always aware that he might be quietly listening in to find out what chatter was going on over the Pye radio. It was a well-known fact that Wing Commander Wills hated unnecessary chatter and insisted that everyone should use the correct R/T language and radio procedure. Sometimes civilian MT drivers, who for various reasons were called upon to drive the CO's Austin 1800, would use his call sign, much to the annoyance of the men in local control. The practice caused a lot of confusion, but it kept everyone on their toes.

The controllers did not necessarily work the same shift pattern as the rest of us, and normally we did not know who we would be working with until we arrived on duty. The main controllers at that time were Flight Lieutenants Clarke, Dawes, Winters and White, while the senior NCOs were Master Pilot Brown, Master Engineer Burns and Flight Sergeant Bob Baker. Flying Officer Jarvis, a former senior NCO, arrived just after me and turned out to be a wonderful controller. Flight Sergeant Bob Kaye, a former Halifax pilot, was only qualified for local control and he refused to go on a radar course because he was soon to retire. Like Bob Kaye, many of the controllers had been pilots or aircrew during the war, but most of them had ceased flying many years ago. In RAF language they were known as 'penguins' because they had 'wings' but they could not fly!

Nothing exciting happened on my first watch, but the months prior to my arrival at Manston had been quite busy, and the 'foam carpet' had been laid on two occasions. The Pyrene Runway Foamer had been introduced at Manston in early 1963, and it was first used by an RAF Valiant, WZ396, which had experienced a main undercarriage failure, forcing the pilot to make a wheels-up landing on 23 May 1964.

In April 1965, the foamer facility had been demonstrated to a large gathering of senior RAF and fire brigade officers, and the first 'official' incident after that was on 7 February 1966 when a Dominie carried out another wheels-up landing. The two foam tanker units sat just a short distance from the main runway, at the top of the western taxiway, and they could be made ready for an emergency in a matter of minutes.

Manston's most famous incident occurred on 27 April 1967 when a British Eagle Bristol Britannia landed on the foam carpet without any wheels at all. The aircraft, G-ANCG, had taken off from Heathrow with fifty-four passengers on board as part of an MoD contract, destined for Adelaide in Australia. After taking off the pilot noticed that the starboard undercarriage leg would not lock, and subsequent attempts to alleviate the problem damaged the hydraulics. After circling the south of England for 5 hours, the pilot elected to land on a foam carpet. The undercarriage collapsed on landing and the fact that nobody was seriously injured was a credit to the skill of the pilots.

On that very same day, another Britannia crashed on the outskirts of Nicosia in Cyprus with the loss of 126 lives. The Globe Air Britannia, Swiss-registered HB-ITB, was orbiting the airfield after making two unsuccessful attempts to land in bad weather. Ironically, it had been diverted to Nicosia because of bad weather at Cairo; it was not a good day to be flying in a Bristol Britannia.

On 30 September 1968 a Dan Air Ambassador, G-AMAG, landed on its belly at Manston without any serious injuries to its passengers or crew, although the aircraft was a write-off. Just a week before I arrived, the foam carpet was laid down once again for an RAF Argosy, whose crew had struggled with a hydraulic failure that prevented the nose wheel from

Monarch Airlines Britannia G-AOVN having made an emergency landing at Manston. It is claimed that this incident took place on 13 June 1972, but I remember a similar thing happening to a Monarch Britannia just before I was posted to Cyprus in May 1971. It was suspected nose wheel failure; the CO strolled up the aircraft and poked in the nose wheel well with his stick! Either the date of this photo is wrong or there were two emergency landings involving Monarch Britannias.

lowering. The aircraft suffered a minimum amount of damage, and it was quickly repaired before being flown back to Benson on 5 November.

After my first shift as the approach controller's assistant, I had been put to work in Movements to learn how to handle signals and Flight Planning. Eventually it was considered that I was knowledgeable enough and ready to work upstairs in local control. The first 'foamer' to be laid after my arrival happened on the first morning that I was assigned to duties as the local controller's assistant.

The incident began when the local controller was contacted via the mini-com system by the approach controller to warn him that a Sea Vixen was short of fuel and there was a red light on the nose wheel, indicating that it was not locked down. It was a desperate situation and after the Aircraft Servicing Flight and MT section had been notified, the two foam tankers began to move towards the runway.

Within minutes, the SATCO and Wing Commander Wills, the station commander, were standing behind me discussing what pattern of foam should be laid. The telephones were ringing repeatedly and messages were being passed backward and forward. With each of the controllers and officers having their own ideas about how to handle the situation there was a lot of tension in the air. Because I lacked experience, when SAC John Scotney came upstairs to enquire about who wanted tea or coffee for the brew, it was suggested that he take over from me from me while I go downstairs to make the brew!

When I arrived back upstairs with a tray full of tea and coffee, I was just in time to see the Sea Vixen approaching from the direction of Acol, to land on runway 11. To begin with, the aircraft seemed to touch down safely, but then the pilot lost control and it ended up skewing off the runway to the right. The Sea Vixen ran uncontrolled across the sterile area and stopped not very far away from the boundary fence on the perimeter of the main Canterbury to Ramsgate road.

Crash 1 reported to the tower over the Pye radio that the Vixen's undercarriage was down, but the aircraft had suffered a hydraulics failure and sustained some minor damage. The 'Meat Wagon', radio call sign Red Cross 1, said that the pilot had been extremely sick and was vomiting, but he was otherwise unhurt. He had been very lucky because we later heard that he had been down to the last few pounds of fuel. When the duty crew at ASF dipped and checked the Vixen's fuel tanks they claimed that there was not enough to fill a cigarette lighter!

By comparison with previous incidents, the Sea Vixen foam landing was only a minor affair, but such excitements happened quite regularly. Hardly a week went by without the pilot of a Canberra, Vulcan or Victor calling us to say that he was experiencing some kind of problem with hydraulics or electrics. Sometime the message would come via a telephone call from Uxbridge or the aircraft's base to check our weather state and tell us that an aircraft had some kind of snag with a wheel or undercarriage.

On other occasions, the aircraft's crew would contact us directly over the UHF/VHF radio and tell us about the problem. The failure to get a green light on the instrument panel to indicate that the wheels were down and locked was the most common cause. Quite often problems were caused by micro-switch failures that were eventually sorted out, so that after the initial call on the radios we never heard any more about it. Sometimes they were caused by what was called 'finger trouble', which was the term used to describe pilot error.

I soon learned that much of what happened in air traffic control was about routine and safety, and airfield inspections were carried out twice a day to check the serviceability of the airfield. First thing in a morning at 6.30 a.m., one of the two shift corporals would drive out onto the airfield in the air traffic Land Rover, call sign 'Rover 1'. He would drive along the taxiways and the down the runways in both directions, looking for any lights that were not working, or for 'FOB', another term to describe anything that might endanger an aircraft. Such objects were often things that were dropped out of vehicles, or on the odd occasion, fallen off aircraft. A similar inspection was carried out during the evening shift, but they could be carried out at any time the local controller chose.

During the evening of 28 November, we had only just started our 15-hour night shift at 5 p.m. when the pilot of a civilian airliner called Manston approach, using the call sign Golf Alpha Tango Golf Delta. A quick scan through the civil registration book told us that this was a Bristol Britannia belonging to Transglobe Airways. The pilot claimed that he was diverting to Manston because of bad weather at Gatwick, but when the controller checked with London Centre they said the weather there was fine. That made everyone a bit suspicious, but within a few minutes the four-engine turboprop Britannia was on final approach.

By now the SATCO had been contacted and he arrived in the tower just as a second civil aircraft called approach to advise the controller that he was also diverting to Manston because of bad weather at his base. This was a Canadair CL 44, G-AWOV, a type that was similar to a Britannia but designed with a tail that swung open for easier access when loading. To begin with, the SATCO said he would not allow it to land, but when the

Transglobe Bristol Britannia G-ATGD, which diverted to Manston when the airline was liquidated in November 1968. The aircraft is sitting on the aircraft servicing platform by the side of the control tower. There is a wonderful view across the airfield of the white houses belong to the officers' married quarters. (*Steve Williams*)

pilot declared an emergency because he was low on fuel, there was nothing that he could do to stop it.

A decision was made to park both the aircraft on the Aircraft Servicing Platform (ASP) by the control tower and within a few minutes the CL 44 followed the Britannia off the northern and down the western taxiway. It was an impressive sight as both aircraft trundled across the main Birchington to Ramsgate road, past lines of traffic that had been halted by the crash fire section. The Britannia was a product of the late 1950s, but the CL 44 was almost brand new and it had only been registered in August 1968 and delivered to Transglobe in October.

Both aircraft were resplendent in the company's dark blue and white colour scheme, with 'Transglobe' painted in large red letters on the fuselage. On the tail was a globe with a thin cross running through it, and the letter 'T' painted in white.

It was soon became clear that Transglobe Airways had collapsed, and the aircraft had been flown to Manston to prevent them being impounded at Gatwick. It was a bad time for Britain's airline industry; Transglobe had collapsed within a month of British Eagle, Britain's major independent airline.

As Invicta Airways normally dealt with large civil aircraft, it immediately offered to handle the CL 44 and Britannia. However, because of the legal situation, their assistance had to be declined. It was a busy night with lots of phone calls from various organisations wanting to know what had happened to the two aircraft. The Aircraft Servicing Flight took over the initial maintenance of the aircraft and made sure that they were properly shut down, chocked and secured. The following day a team of engineers from Gatwick arrived to carry out basic maintenance, and ensure that the aircraft were properly secured.

Although we did not know it at the time, the Britannia and CL 44 were to become long-term residents, and the job of calculating the parking fees, like many other boring duties, fell to me. I had to calculate the on-going parking fees and then transfer the amounts on to the RAF Form 2920, which was filed in triplicate. Then it had to be double checked by Corporal Budd or Sergeant Sheldrake in the office. 'Paper pushing' was never my favourite occupation.

Manston was regularly visited by a number of civilian aircraft that were flown by well-known personalities. Hughie Green, the quizmaster of shows like 'Double Your Money' and 'Opportunity Knocks', owned a Cessna 337 Skymaster, G-ASLL. He had been a ferry pilot during the war and had flown a large number of transport aircraft across the Atlantic. Hughie also had a large boat tied up in Ramsgate Harbour, and he was a regular visitor to Margate where he drank at the Elephant and Castle.

Douglas Bader also flew in on a number of occasions, and he maintained his reputation for being quite stubborn. He would never let anyone carry his bags or assist him, and he would shout and swear at anyone who tried to help him. The wing commander was too well respected for anyone to argue with him; most airmen just kept out of his way and let him get on with things the way he wanted.

The other regular members of my watch were Senior Aircraftsman Dave Smith, Hughie O'Neal, John Scotney and Denis Todd, all of whom were married and lived in married quarters. Corporal Peter Turner could be quite serious at times, especially when it came to music, but I soon found out that he liked a laugh as much as anyone else. When he was not manning the runway caravan, he would mess about like the rest of us. He liked to tell me stories about things that had happened at Manston before I arrived.

One of his is favourite tales was about a night when he was carrying out an airfield inspection and he came across a car towing a caravan down the main runway. Peter claimed that the driver was totally unaware of where he was and the fact that a large aircraft might land on top of him at any minute. It turned out that somebody from the crash fire section had inadvertently left the crash gate open on the Canterbury Road close to the Prospect Inn, near the end of the runway 11. In misty conditions, the elderly male driver, who was probably totally disorientated, had driven through it, thinking it was some new kind of lighting. He thought that he was still on the main road that runs parallel to the runway, and he was astounded to see so many multicoloured bright lights! Many years later, Peter confirmed that what he had told me was true, but admitted that over time, the story might have become a bit embellished!

Another anecdote concerned Corporal Brian Atkinson, who was on another shift to us. He was out in the runway caravan one day when he was asked to bring it back to the control tower, where it was to be collected by an MT driver for routine maintenance. As he drove up to the tower, Brian was probably thinking that he was still driving the air traffic Land-Rover, and he attempted to park it in the bay on the far side of the building. Unfortunately, it was not high enough for the runway caravan to clear the overhang, and the subsequent collision resulted in the glass dome being totally demolished. The incident would not have done his assessments any good, but I understood that he got off lightly without being charged.

The other corporal on my shift was 'Robbie' Robinson. He ran the 'Tea Swindle', a tariff of 2/- a week for the tea and coffee that everyone drank in large amounts. Robbie was married and lived in quarters, while Peter Turner was single and lived in the block. Being a southerner and from Ilford, Peter hated all northerners, and he used to tease me terribly about coming from Manchester, where he claimed it was always raining. Generally it was all a bit of banter, and although the insults sometimes got a bit serious, nobody got too upset.

We all got on reasonably well, although there were huge differences in age and experience between me and the other members of the shift. It was claimed that Hughie O'Neil was the oldest airman in the RAF; he was probably thirty years my senior and we often clashed over the most trivial matters. Dave Smith was of a slight build and a keen basketball player; he played for both Manston and the Coastal Command Teams. Denis Todd was originally from Burma and at one time he had been a pilot flying Vickers Viscounts, but he had been taken off flying when it had been found that he had a problem with his eyesight. Denis, John Scotney and Ron Sadler were all keen members of the Royal Antidiluvian Order of The Buffaloes and they were making plans to set up a lodge on the camp at Manston.

Most arguments during a shift were caused when we played cards in the evening. 'Clag', an RAF variation of the game 'Brag', was the favourite game in air traffic. There were always accusations of cheating and although we played only for a few pence (match sticks for pennies), things sometimes got highly charged. We also frequently disagreed about whose turn it was to be 'stood down' on the night watch.

During or before a night shift (5 p.m.–8 a.m.), the duty controller told the corporal of the watch how many airmen he required, and normally at least one airman and a corporal were stood down. On most occasions, those who stood down did not even have to turn up for the watch, but officially they were required to be on call and available if needed. This was all done on an unofficial basis and no lists or names were kept, but it was normal practice that the airman who had stayed up all night on the previous shift got stood down on the next one. Only one airman remained awake and alert while the others slept down in Flight Planning or in the SATCO's office. They were awoken at 6.30 a.m., with a cup of tea and often the welcoming call, 'It's time to get up, you lazy bastards!'

CHAPTER 7

Ghosts of the Past

Like many other RAF stations, RAF Manston has a long and illustrious history. It came into being in 1916 with the closure of the Royal Navy's seaplane base at St Mildred's Bay, near Westgate. The base had been situated close to Margate's eighteenth-century sea bathing hospital, but after a number of accidents, it was decided that a safer site needed to be found inland.

The pilots of RNAS Westgate saw a lot of action and total of seven airmen were killed. The first casualty was 23-year-old Sub Lieutenant Reginald Lord, who was killed on 10 August 1915. Lord was flying a Sopwith Tabloid and he was returning at night from a sortie to intercept the Zeppeln L12. He misjudged his approach and crashed into the ground, dying in hospital shortly after.

Lord was an exceptionally talented pilot who had gone solo after only 2 hours and 35 minutes, but there was no evidence to suggest that enemy action was responsible for his accident. He was from a prominent Northumberland family and his grandfather was the Mayor of Newcastle, but he was buried in Margate Cemetery. He was one of the first among many servicemen from both wars to be buried at Margate.

In early 1920, a technical training school (later Number 3 School of T.T.) was established at Manston to train unskilled and semi-skilled workers such as clerks, butchers and cooks. The pattern of the station evolved to serve and accommodate that unit, and some of the building survives to the present day. The two-storey 'H' block buildings and the lines of single-storey concrete buildings were still being used until the 1990s. The area surrounding the old parade ground became the football pitch.

There were many myths and legends about things that had happened at Manston over the years, and the ambiance in certain areas of the station made the hair on the back of one's neck stand up. Rather typically, there were many tales concerning ghost, the paranormal and other unexplained events. One of those that I heard early on concerned an airman who had been killed in a freak incident involving a helicopter on the western taxiway. When some people walked around that area at night, they often got the feeling that they were being watched.

It was not until May 2006 that I discovered the truth behind this incident, while being shown around Margate Cemetery by one of its trustees, Mr John Williams. When we arrived at the grave of LAC Allan Wilkes Rae, John explained that this airman had been killed in an incident at Manston on 2 November 1960. That information sent a little shiver down my spine, especially when John explained that he had been killed in a freak accident involving a helicopter, in almost exactly the same circumstances as I had heard many years ago. I was slightly shocked to discover that what for many years had been just another urban myth, was in fact based on a true story, regardless of whether there was a ghost or not!

One morning, having completed a night shift and had breakfast in the airmen's mess, I was on my way back to the block when I came across the NAAFI manager, Charlie Seagar. He was walking down the road from the sergeants' mess, dressed in his trousers with his pyjama top sticking out and looking quite distressed. He said that he had hardly slept that night because someone or something had been knocking on the door of his flat for most of the night. To begin with he had thought that it was the usual rabble messing about on the outside corridor, but then he realised the noise was actually coming from the inner door. The outer door to the corridor was locked and there had been no sign of a physical presence outside or inside this room that could explain what Charlie thought he had heard.

Charlie was a 'down to earth' man from Burnley who had seen a great many things in his time. He was also a man of the world and not easily frightened, but this incident and other subsequent unexplained events in his flat shook him up a great deal. He later did some research into the rooms that he lived in and discovered that during the war, a wing commander had committed suicide while living there. Other than those facts, nothing else was ever found out!

It was also claimed that the officers' mess building was haunted by a ghost who was commonly referred to as the 'White Lady' because she allegedly appeared as a white apparition. The building had been an old farmhouse on Pouces Farm that had formed part of the original site on which the airfield had been built. The farmhouse was said date from the seventeenth century. One on occasion during the early hours of one morning, when I was on duty in the control tower, Flight Lieutenant 'Chalky' White turned up unexpectedly, carrying all his bedding in his arms.

He was the orderly officer that night, and as per regulations, he was supposed to have slept in the officer's mess annex, but he claimed his sleep had been disturbed several times by some strange eerie apparition entering his room. In the end, he could stand it no longer, and gave up his bed and spent the night in the armchair in the approach room.

During the Second World War, over 3,000 RAF servicemen were based at Manston, a huge number compared to the 100 or so stationed there in 1968. Such was the threat of invasion in 1940, it is claimed that Winston Churchill personally ordered a flight of Spitfires to fly above Thanet every morning, to assure local people that they had not been abandoned.

However, the RAF could not prevent Manston, Margate, Ramsgate or any other town from coming under attack. On 24 August 1940, the Luftwaffe got through to make one of its most devastating raids. Twenty Heinkel 111s

Prime Minister Winston Churchill visiting 615 Squadron personnel on 28 August 1940. The unit was based at Kenley, but had a detachment at Manston.

bypassed Dover and dropped sixty bombs on Ramsgate Airport and another 150 on the town itself. The attack lasted just five minutes, but the results were devastating and many people were killed or injured.

The first time I became aware of what an important role Manston had played during the Battle of Britain was on the first occasion that I was assigned to the role of duty airman. At the end of the working day, the duty airman had to take down the flag from station headquarters, and then make sure that all the doors and windows of the building were secured. It was while I was checking the station commander's office that I came across the 'Manston Score 1941–45' – a small wooden board that detailed the number of enemy aircraft and ships destroyed by aircraft based at Manston.

The board was divided into six different categories, one for each of the main squadrons that had operated out of the airfield during the relevant period of the war. Represented were 605 Squadron equipped with Mosquitos; 609 Squadron equipped with Typhoons; 406 Squadron equipped also with Mosquitos; 137 Squadron equipped with Whirlwinds, Hurricanes and Typhoons; 198 Squadron equipped with Typhoons; and 3 Squadron

A line up of 3 Squadron pilots at Manston. The unit was based at Manston on two occasions from June to December 1943. It was then equipped with Hurricanes, but by the time it returned to Manston in February 1944, it had re-equipped with Typoons and Tempests, and was credited with destroying a number of flying bombs.

equipped with Hurricanes and Typhoons. The board detailed the number of aircraft destroyed in the air and on the ground, and the number of flying bombs destroyed; the station's total for the latter was 165.

Strangely enough, the scoreboard fails to mention the contribution of 501 Squadron, which moved to Manston on 2 August 1944 and was equipped with Hawker Tempests under the command of Squadron Leader Joe Berry DFC. While it was operating from Manston, 501 Squadron was among the units that destroyed the highest number of V-1s, and Squadron Leader Berry was later credited with sixty-one flying bombs destroyed, nearly twice the number of any other pilot.

To put Squadron Leader Berry's achievement into perspective, the next highest scorer was Flight Lieutenant Mellersh who flew with 96 Squadron and was credited with forty-seven flying bombs destroyed. Third on the role of honour was Wing Commander Roland Beamont with forty-one. Not only is 501 Squadron not mentioned on the Manston scoreboard, but the Tempest is not listed as a type of aircraft that flew from the airfield.

There is a mystery concerning Squadron Leader Berry that has sinister overtones. Just before 501 Squadron moved to Bradwell Bay, a senior officer took one of the squadron's Tempests up into the air on a sortie without asking his permission. Despite the fact that the other senior officer was a group captain, Squadron Leader Berry gave him a 'severe ticking off', but made the mistake of doing it in front of an audience of airmen and other officers.

Just before he was killed on 2 October 1944, Squadron Leader Berry wrote a letter to his sister telling her about the incident. He told her that the officer had made it clear that he was not happy with what had happened and he was going to send Squadron Leader Berry and 501 Squadron on a special operation to teach him a lesson. The letter does not disclose the identity of the officer concerned.

Twenty-four-year-old Squadron Leader Berry was killed on 2 October 1944 when his Tempest EJ 600 was hit by flak while flying in on a dawn ranger sortie, south-west of Assen in Holland. Flying at only 50 feet he stood little chance of bailing out of his aircraft. He was accompanied by two other 501 Squadron Tempests, flown by Flight Lieutenants 'Willy' Williams and 'Horry' Hanson. His last words were reported as being, 'I've had it chaps … you go on,' and seconds later his aircraft flipped over on its back and crashed into the ground in Kibbelgaan, a small hamlet 4½ miles south of Sheemda. He was buried in the village by the school master and some other local people who risked their lives in paying their respects to a British airman whose name they did not even know.

During the war, just down the road from Manston was one of the most important radar stations on the south coast, RAF Sandwich. It was a Ground Controlled Interception (GCI) station that had been originally set up at Willesborough near Ashford with Type 8b Radar. Because the Germans regularly jammed its signals, the site was moved to Sandwich in 1942. Situated close to the second-century Roman fort of Richborough, the Sandwich GCI station became fully operational with the Type 7 Radar in April 1943. The large rotating aerial fed information to the operations block, and it controlled the interceptions of enemy aircraft over the whole of the south-east of England.

By the end of the war, Sandwich was staffed by eighty-seven airmen and officers and 154 WAAFs. Over the years it went through a number of changes. It became part of the ROTOR Air Defence Network, and under the name 'Ash Radar', it provided an important air traffic control facility that covered the approaches from the coast to London's airports. The site remained operational until 1974 when its role was taken over by the modern air traffic facilities at West Drayton.

From July 1950 until June 1958, Manston was occupied by various fighter and bomber wings of the United States Air Force. Even the Americans had some strange experiences, although with UFOs rather than ghosts! On 20 May 1957, 25-year-old Lieutenant John Milton Torres was one of two pilots scrambled from Manston to pursue an unidentified aircraft over East Anglia.

Torres belonged to the 514th Fighter Interceptor Squadron that was equipped with the F 86. Once the aircraft were airborne they were vectored onto their target by ground radar units. Torres and his wingman were ordered to engage re-heat, and to be prepared to fire their twenty-four fin-tailed rockets. They soon picked the contact up on their radar. The 'blip' was so powerful that Torres later said it was going to burn a hole in his screen. He described the size of the contact as that of a flying aircraft carrier. When flying at 761 mph, awaiting orders to confirm they were to open fire, the blip suddenly disappeared.

The two F 86s returned safely to Manston where the pilots were debriefed on what they had encountered. Torres claimed that during the pursuit he had an overwhelming feeling that had they fired their rockets their aircraft would have been 'vaporised'. He estimated that whatever it was that they were chasing was flying at 7,000 mph and capable of carrying out manoeuvres that no earth-based aircraft could ever attempt. So as not to cause alarm the incident was classified as 'Secret' and details of it were not released until October 2008.

As a young airman serving at Manston in 1969, I could sometimes reach out and feel the history that surrounded me at every turn. The station had a strange and unique atmosphere that I had never experienced before, but that was hardly surprising given the fact that the whole area had witnessed so much bloodshed and violence. After dark the station seemed to come alive, with the wind carrying the whispers and voices across the airfield in flickering shadows. Maybe I just had a vivid imagination, but at the time it was often very scary!

In May 1968 the 'enemy' returned to Manston when two Heinkel bombers, accompanied by fifteen Messerschmitt 109s, arrived from across the English Channel. One by one they wheeled overhead and landed at the airfield; the swastikas and crosses brought fear into the hearts of those locals who had been around back in 1940. However, there was no reason to be concerned. The aircraft were passing through Manston to be inspected by the Air Registration Board, prior to them taking part in the film 'The Battle of Britain'. It would not be the last time that the Luftwaffe would visit Manston, and its presence always raised powerful emotions!

CHAPTER 8

New Experiences

One thing I soon learned about at Manston was that pay parades like those at Swinderby were non-existent, and although the official payday was Thursday, there was normally a casual pay 'parade' on Tuesday. This was partly because most airmen worked shifts and were not always available to collect their money on Thursdays, but also because of the partial recognition that the authorities knew that our pay could not last until the end of the week.

Like everything else at Manston, whatever the day of the week, collecting one's pay was a very casual affair; all we had to do was to turn up in the accounts office at or after 11 a.m. The accounts officer, or whoever was around, would just check our ID (most of them knew who we were anyway), and hand over the cash. The only formality was that we had to sign for it. It was a totally different experience to that at basic training where we had to salute and virtually beg for our pay. Everyone in the accounts office at Manston was very friendly.

One occasion that comes to mind was when I was told to report for casual pay parade with a Corporal Blackman, whom I had never heard of before. When I arrived in the accounts office there was only one person there, a young black guy sitting in his shirt sleeves.

'Can I help you?' he asked. I said that I had been told to report to Corporal Blackman and I asked if he was in the office. The account's clerk looked puzzled. Screwing his face up and pretending to look under his desk he said, 'You're looking for Corporal Blackman? Let me ask you, how many black men do you see around here?... I am he ... Corporal Blackman!'

In most cases the attitude and humour of service personnel would make nonsense of modern political correctness. Pete Blackman subsequently became a good friend.

The winter of 1968-69 was a particularly cold one, and the boiler that heated the sergeants' mess and airmen's accommodation was often broken, leaving the accommodation blocks icily cold. Some airmen had electric fires in their rooms, but officially they were not allowed. Besides, I had not been organised enough to get one so I just suffered the cold.

One particularly cold night after leaving the warmth of the NAAFI bar, I was offered a hot drink by an airman called John who lived in a room across the corridor. He had a powerful two-bar electric fire in his room. As he made the drinks he put on some music and we casually began to talk about life at Manston. It was all very cosy and pleasant, but I suddenly noticed that John was getting very touchy feely, in fact more feely than touchy as he began to rub my knee gently with his hand.

As his hand moved from my knee towards my thigh the sudden realisation of what he was up to made me jump up and shout a number of expletives. I was very embarrassed and I muttered that I was 'not like that' and then in something of a fluster I fled from his room. Once in the security of my own space, I locked the door but I told no one about my experience until some weeks later, when one night after a few drinks in the NAAFI bar, another new arrival, Jim, began to talk of a similar encounter. His inhibitions were loosened by several pints of beer and it soon became clear that his experience involved the very same person. I was very much relieved to hear what some of the old hands had to say about it.

Bill Newman who was an electrician on the Aircraft Servicing Flight joined in the conversation and he told us in no uncertain terms that John was not a homosexual, but just trying to 'work his ticket'. This was a new term to me, but he explained that if we had reported John for what he had done, then there was a good chance that he might be thrown out of the air force. Bill said that was what John was hoping for, and apparently he had tried it on before with other new arrivals without any success. In future, John would try various other means to try to ensure that he was discharged, but he gave up on pretending to be a homosexual.

There were quite a few characters at Manston, but Bill Newman, with his dry sense of humour and cutting witty remarks made in his off-beat Scouse accent, was one of the most notorious. Although everyone thought he was a Scouser, Bill actually came from Ellesmere Port, and he was very proud of his Merseyside roots. He was small and stocky, and often worked out with his 'Bullworker' machine to keep himself fit.

In another age Bill would have been called one of the 'Gen Men', and he always had the answer to any problem that one might have, be it service related or of a personal nature. Not long after I arrived at Manston, the government began to jam pirate radio stations like Radio Caroline, which was broadcast from a ship in the English Channel. Most of us listened regularly to Caroline and preferred it to the drab music of BBC Radio 1. It was not long before Bill came up with the answer; he discovered that if we wrapped our radios in tin foil and pointed the aerial in the direction of the coast, the jamming was 'jammed', and we could still hear the pirate stations. Result: Bill Newman 1 Government 0!

It is hard to believe in this age of the internet and mobile phones that in 1969, the year the Americans put a man on the moon, the only means of making contact with the outside world was via a red telephone box situated by the side of the guard room. STD was only slowly being introduced across the UK, and most long distance routes involved what were known as 'trunk calls', which meant going through an operator.

There was an STD line in the movements room of the control tower, and when we were on duty we could make outside calls, but it was strictly against orders to use it for non-official business. The number was THANET 51641 and it was often passed around to girlfriends and family members who would ring during the evening and ask to be put through to their loved ones. Anyone else who wanted to contact us had to ring the number of the main switchboard, Manston 351, and ask to be connected to the number of whatever extension we were on.

I soon found out that there were a number of jobs at Manston that were left specially for the 'new boy', and not all of them involved making tea and coffee. One of them involved turning around the large white wooden letter 'T' in the signal's square when the wind swung around and the duty controller decided to change the runway in use. The crossbar of the letter pointed towards the direction of runway, which was either 11 or 29, and although the system was obsolete, it still had to be done even when there was bad visibility and heavy rain.

Another unwelcome task was cleaning the windows of local control, and the big glass-topped dome at the top of the control tower. Given a squeegee, a bucket of warm water and a set of steps, one was expected to wash each frame of glass until the local controller was satisfied that it had been done properly. However, it always turned out that no matter how clean the glass was, either an officer or senior NCO would point out a bit that had been missed or smeared. Cleaning the windows was a particularly thankless task, and for some strange reason it always rained shortly afterwards anyway!

Manston's control tower, whitewashed as I remember it, before it was changed to a horrible brown colour scheme.

Despite these and other irksome duties that I had to perform, I settled in at Manston quite well. I soon got myself a girlfriend (a nurse at Margate Sea Bathing Hospital), and so I was less keen to go home to Manchester. Subsequently, my long-standing girlfriend at home became rather suspicious by my absence! However, I did still make the occasional visit home both to keep the peace and my options open.

Because I could rarely afford the rail fare, unless I had a travel warrant my favourite mode of transport between Manchester and London was the overnight coach. The North-Western coach left Manchester's Mosley Street Bus Station just after midnight, and it arrived at Victoria at 7.30 a.m., just in time for me to connect with the Ramsgate train. On one occasion, however, on a Friday night when the coach was full of Manchester City fans going to an away game in London, the coach broke down. We all had had to wait several hours for a relief coach to arrive while they sang their heads off. For a Manchester United fan it was a very unpleasant experience!

During my first few months at Manston, Margate was the place that I visited most regularly and in particular the Bally Hai Bar that was part of the Dreamland complex. My friend Paddy was very popular with the ladies and within a few minutes of entering the bar in Dreamland on the first night I went out with him, he had talked two girls into coming over and having a drink with us. Angela and Susan were student nurses who worked at Margate's sea bathing hospital. After a few more drinks they invited us back to their rooms at the Nurses' Home for 'coffee'.

It was a lot easier getting into the Nurses' Home than it was getting out the following morning, with lots of nurses coming off the night shift and others going on duty. It was like a military operation trying to sneak out without being seen, and it was a great relief to be finally back at Manston.

In a letter to my parents on 2 December, I told them that I was well and that I had begun working for Invicta Airlines. I said that the previous Saturday night I had helped to load aircraft bound for Biafra with ammunition. The aircraft in question were CL 44s belonging to a company called Tradewinds; they were carrying out regular flights at night to Nigeria in support of its regime that was fighting the breakaway state of Biafra, which had declared independence on 3 June 1967.

The flights took an average of 15 hours and we had to write out the flight plans – something of a nightmare as French air traffic controllers were on strike again! Many of the flights had to be routed out via the Atlantic, and that meant the pilots had to get an 'Oceanic' clearance as well as their normal airways clearance before they could proceed.

One night the cargo they carried would be medical supplies bound for Lagos in southern Nigeria, and the next night it could be ammunition bound for Kano in the north. We would load ammunition in the form of .762 bullets, which were stored in brown metal boxes and packed in large wooden crates piled up inside Invicta's black hangar. British aid to Nigeria to suppress Biafra was to become a very controversial issue, but we got paid 6/6 an hour for our labour.

The flights continued for some time and a number of other companies were involved as the war raged on until 15 January 1970. This work was the start of my connection with Invicta Airlines and many of those who worked in air traffic control moonlighted on the other side of the airfield. There was a long association between the RAF and the civil airlines that had begun when Air Ferry had flown from Manston. It was not just a means of extra income, but a social bond; there was a lot of ribaldry between Invicta's employees and ourselves. Invicta's managing director, Hugh Kennard, was himself a former RAF wing commander who had commanded one of the 'Eagle' squadrons made up of American personnel. At the end of the war he ended up as the commanding officer of RAF Hawkinge, an airfield near Folkestone that had long wartime associations with Fighter Command.

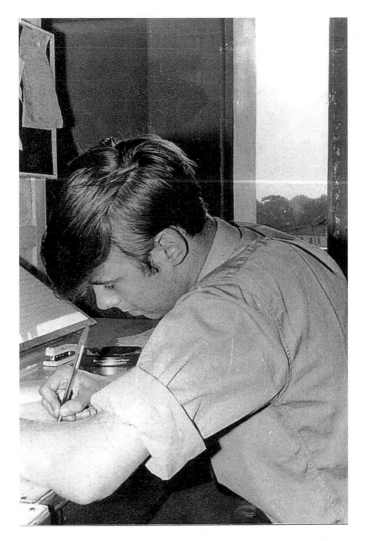

The author at work writing out a flight plan in the movements room of RAF Manston's control tower. The door by the notice board leads to the SATCO's office and through the window you can just see the station headquarters building.

There were regular complaints about Invicta's pilots failing to respect routine air traffic procedures and how they took it for granted that they could move about the airfield freely. Before starting the engines it was standard practice for pilots to call the control tower on the frequency of 124.9 and ask for 'start up clearance'. Then they had to request 'taxi clearance' to the runway or holding point of whatever runway was in use. On many occasions, Invicta's DC 4s would be on the northern taxiway before the pilot called the tower. Sometimes they would anger controllers at London Air Traffic Control Centre (ATCC) by requesting an airways clearance when their operations had not even submitted a flight plan. It was flying on a shoe string, Invicta fashion!

As the Christmas of 1968 approached, Corporal Budd and Sergeant Sheldrake asked for volunteers to work over the stand down period. I was told that it was customary for single airmen to work Christmas so that married airmen could spend the time with their families. I have always been keener to celebrate the New Year than Christmas, and so I had no objection to working Christmas Day. There were no movements at all, but the weather boards had to be maintained just in case. The only signal we received was to confirm that one of Invicta's DC 4s had arrived safely in Australia with a cargo of oil pipes. We spent most of the time watching the television in the movements room, and we were allowed the occasional alcoholic beverage to help the Christmas spirit!

There were a number of changes in January 1969 and the station commander, Wing Commander D. B. Wills DFC, was replaced by Wing Commander E. N. Scott AFM. Wing Commander Wills had served at Manston since November 1965 and had pioneered the foam landing facility. He had been involved with the first major incidents such as the British Eagle Britannia.

On the civil side there was also a major change; Invicta Airlines announced a planned merger with British Midland Airways, based at Castle Donnington in Derbyshire. Invicta's fleet of three DC 4s and two Vickers Viscounts were amalgamated into two separate companies that operated passengers and freight. The passenger side was renamed British Midland and its new fleet consisted of twelve Viscounts, while the freight operation continued to utilise the three DC 4s and was to be called British Midland – Invicta Air Cargo. It was not exactly a marriage made in heaven.

It was announced at about the same time that the helicopters of 22 Squadron 'D' Flight would be withdrawn from Manston at the end of March. The squadron was equipped with Whirlwind Mk X helicopters, which provided an air sea rescue facility along what was one of the busiest

An Invicta Airways Viscount and, behind it, a DC 4, the workhorse of the Invicta fleet. When this photograph was taken in September 1968, the DC 4 had virtually disappeared from the British Register. Invicta, however, had three of them – G-ASEN, G-ASPM and G-ASPM – and the type was in service until the 1972. Invicta had two Viscounts – G-AOCB and G-AOCC – but it also operated a number of others in conjunction with British Midland Airways. Invicta and British Midland merged in early 1969; when the merge failed all the Viscounts went back to British Midland.

stretches of coast in the world. They had been based at Manston since July 1961, and had saved a huge number of stricken crews during their eight years' service. Despite a campaign being launched by the local newspapers and Thanet District Council to keep the helicopters at Manston, the deadline was set for the withdrawal.

The sea lanes were only to get busier and on 17 January, Hoverlloyd began trials with the giant SRN4 hovercraft from the new £1 million hoverport at Pegwell Bay. The SRN4 could carry 254 passengers and thirty cars, and they were a lot bigger than the thirty-six-seat SRN6 hovercraft that Hoverlloyd had operated out of Ramsgate Harbour since April 1966. The hoverport in Pegwell Bay at Cliffsend was a dedicated terminal building with its own access road and engineering facilities.

On 23 January, the first of Hoverlloyd's SRN4 hovercraft was officially named 'Swift' by the wife of the Prime Minister, Mary Wilson. The hoverport was not opened officially for another four months, but it was the beginning of the service to Calais Harbour.

Shortly after the hoverport opened, I went with two airmen and a civilian, a meteorologist called Tim, to spend a couple of days in France. The idea was that we would live like French peasants, eating just bread and cheese and drinking lots of wine. Neil Taylor, who had recently arrived at Manston, owned a left-hand-drive Volkswagen camper van that he had purchased in Germany. Although he had only recently joined the RAF and was just a leading aircraftsman, his father was a squadron leader. Because his father was an officer, we were a bit suspicious of him to begin with, but he quickly proved to us that he was one of the boys. He was mad about vehicles of all sorts and was in the process of converting a bread van into another camper van.

Originally there were only the two of us going on the trip, but then Tim the weather man said he would like join us, and because he was the only one who spoke French, he was invited along. Geordie more or less invited himself, and none of us really knew him because he had only recently been posted in. He had just got married and he appeared to be poverty stricken because he always wore his RAF-issue shoes and trousers off duty. The others felt sorry for him and invited him along, but we knew it was going to be a tight squeeze with four of us trying to sleep in one small van.

The forty-minute flight, yes flight, because that was what trips in a hovercraft were called, went quite smoothly, but despite that I was sick! After arriving at Calais, Neil decided that we would drive along the west coast road to Cape Griz-Nez to have a look at some Second World War German bunkers. It felt really strange to be standing where Hitler and Goering had stood just less than thirty years before in anticipation of an invasion of the south coast of England.

By the time we had had a good look around it was early afternoon and we decided to move on before it got too late. It was suggested that we drive east towards Dunkirk to have a look at the beaches where British troops had been evacuated in May 1940.

We got lost in Dunkirk, but then Neil turned down a road signed for the harbour. All of a sudden it became clear that our road was getting narrower with every yard and what we had presumed to be a highway was now no more than a narrow track leading to the pier head! It was clear that we could go no further because we had the sea on both sides and in front of us lay a huge bulk tanker and more water! As we drove back up the way we had come we saw the picket post for the first time. The barrier was down and the two policemen who were standing besides it raised their hands, clearly wanting us to stop.

One of the gendarmes shouted something in French, while gesticulating wildly with his arms.

'What does he want?' Neil asked Tim.

'I'm not sure but I think he wants to know where we have come from.'

'Tell him we're English', shouted Geordie, 'we fought the ★★★★★★★ war for them.'

By now the gendarme was getting quite excited, 'Shut up, Geordie,' said Neil, 'What's he saying, Tim?'

'He wants to know ... how we got here and what ship we came off? He also wants to know why, if we're English, our vehicle is left-hand drive with German registration plates?'

'Because I bought the bloody thing in Germany,' said Neil.

Tim quickly tried to explain, but he was obviously having difficulties. 'I've told him that we came on the hovercraft ... but he doesn't believe me. He says the hoverport is miles away the other side of Calais!'

Before we knew what was happening, the camper van was surrounded by two or three other gendarmes who made it very clear that we were to get out. Tim said that they wanted to see our passports and documentation and we were allowed back into the van to scramble through our bags. When we produced our Hoverlloyd tickets the gendarme seemed even more confused and showed them to his colleagues. They wanted Neil to show a receipt for the vehicle or least proof of ownership; there was a lot of chatter between Tim and the gendarmes in garbled broken French.

Then it suddenly became clear to Tim what had happened; we had entered a restricted customs area. What Neil had taken to be a road was actually the quayside and we had driven past the picket post that controlled access to the docks. We had not seen it when we drove past because a lorry had stopped by the side of it and blocked the view, so that Neil thought it was just another road!

The gendarmes were still not happy because Neil had no proof of ownership, but at least they let us go on our way, albeit grudgingly. After our confusing encounter with the French police, we cut our losses and drove back to Calais where we had something to eat, before visiting a few bars in the evening. We parked up in the main square in Calais close to the old bell tower, where it was very convenient for the shops and bars.

We did not see any point in moving the van and so we bedded down the best we could for a good night's sleep, or at least rest. There were arms and legs everywhere and the smell of sweaty socks and stale beer filled the air, but within a short while, the sound of snoring suggested that everyone had fallen asleep.

All was well until in the early hours of the morning, when we were awoken by a harsh rapping noise on the window of the van. Through bleary eyes we saw the shape of two gendarmes peering in at us, intent on getting our attention. This time we did not need Tim to translate because the gendarme spoke perfect English, or more to the point, he shouted it very loud! He told us in no uncertain terms that it was not allowed for vehicles to park overnight and for people to sleep in them. If we did not move immediately we would be arrested for contravening the by-laws and the vehicle would be impounded.

'The bloody French have got it in for us!' exclaimed Geordie.

For what remained of the night we drove around Calais, trying to avoid the attention of the gendarmes. We went back to the main square near the bell tower but they were waiting for us and we drove off again in a hurry. For about another hour we drove aimlessly about Calais, but then we noticed that a light had appeared in a café across the square and we stopped to see whether it was open. It turned out that the owner was an Englishman and he was very pleased to see us. We breakfasted on egg and chips with lots of toast and a pot of tea thrown in, while listening to the BBC Light Programme.

Neil reluctantly decided that we should quit while we were ahead and get the first available hovercraft back to Ramsgate; the trip had not gone as planned and everyone was getting fed up. We were not due to leave until the afternoon, but we managed to change our tickets without too much fuss, which left us time to wander around the duty free shop. I decided to spend my last few pounds on a bottle of Johnny Walker Black Label and some French bread that smelt freshly baked and wonderful.

I had left it a bit late and all of a sudden someone shouted to me to hurry up because we were about to board the hovercraft. As I struggled to find my boarding card I pushed my way through some large double doors, but someone else came through from the other side making the door swing back into me; I lost my grip on the plastic bag with the whisky and bread in it, and before I knew what was happening, the bottle had fallen to the ground and smashed, and the baguettes were squashed and broken!

I could not believe what had happened, and I stood in shock as the precious liquid ran all over the floor and my shoes. A member of staff tried to help and told me that I had time to go back to the shop if I hurried, but I could hardly think of what to do. I could not afford another bottle of whisky so I picked up a bottle of Dubonet and ran for the departure gate, still clutching the two broken baguettes of French bread that hung limp in the middle. By now the magic of the trip had all but disappeared and I just wanted to get back to England!

Once we were seated and on our way, we all ordered drinks that were delivered to our seats almost straight away; during the forty-minute flight I consumed several tins of beer. Then as we approached Pegwell Bay I suddenly began to feel very warm. The cabin was overwhelmingly stuffy as there was no ventilation. Through the windows and beneath the spray from the sea I could actually see land and the white cliffs near Ramsgate, but they did not seem to get be getting any closer.

I held out for as long as I could, but then I suddenly had an overwhelming urge to grab a sick bag. I began to vomit into it just as the hovercraft rode up onto the ramp. Another minute and I would have been alright, but as it was I suffered the ridicule heaped on me by my three colleagues who had no sympathy whatsoever. For me, the incidents with the customs officers, the French police, the loss of a bottle of whisky and me being sick had somewhat spoiled what should have been a pleasant few days in France. There were no more trips to France, organised or otherwise, and shortly afterwards Neil was posted out.

During my off-duty periods back at Manston, I had other things to occupy my time, such as my ambition to learn how to drive. However, my plans to take to the road were scuttled almost as soon as I got my new provisional driving licence. It all came about because I had arranged to meet my girlfriend Susan in Margate, where I was due to pick her up at the Nurses' Home. Unfortunately, I overslept after working the night shift and a lunchtime drinking session in the NAAFI. I didn't wake up until 6.30 p.m., when I had to be at Margate Sea Bathing Hospital by 7 p.m.

My old friend and neighbour Paddy came to my rescue by suggesting that he could give me a lift into Margate on his motorbike, a BSA 250, that he had recently rebuilt in the motor club workshop. The fact that he had not completed the job did not bother either him or me, and the lack of various essential components went unnoticed. Within a few minutes we were approaching Margate's seafront, and as we turned left by the clock tower, I noticed that a police panda car was parked there.

As we ran along the front towards the railway station I turned around to see that the police car was following us; it soon pulled out beside us and indicated for Paddy to stop. Paddy applied the brakes but had some difficulty in getting the bike to stop; by the time that he did we were on the station approach road. The policeman then got out of his car and strolled over to where we stood, staring at the bike in disbelief! To begin with, he did not speak and just stood shaking his head.

'I'm just going to take this thing apart and do you for every single breach of the law!' he said. He would have had his work cut out, but he did inspect the motorbike very thoroughly and made various entries in his notebook before he wrote down our names and addresses. We were in trouble enough, but when he asked Paddy to produce his driving license and insurance, our position went from bad to worse; Paddy only held a provisional licence!

By this time a crowd of commuters and passers by had gathered, but they did not distract the policeman from his duty. He pointed out that it was illegal for a provisional licence holder to drive a motorbike carrying a passenger unless he also held a full license. I didn't have a license, and in any case, it was illegal to drive without insurance. The bike wasn't even roadworthy! He pointed out that apart from the obvious faults such as there being no 'L' plates, the front light was hanging off, the seat was not fixed properly, the brakes did not work, and there were no pillion foot-rests.

Every little defect was entered into the policeman's note book, and he smiled as he informed us that we would receive a summons in the post during next few weeks. To add to Paddy's frustration, the policeman impounded the motorbike and he said that we would have to walk to wherever we were going! It was not bad for me because the sea bathing hospital was just down the road. Paddy had to take a taxi to return to Manston in time for a nightshift!

A few weeks later we received our summons through the post, ordering us to appear before Margate Magistrates Court. Paddy was charged with various offences relating to driving an un-roadworthy vehicle without having the correct documentation. I was charged with 'aiding and abetting' him to carry out the alleged offences, which came as quite a shock.

We had to tell our appropriate Commanding Officer, which meant another interview with the SATCO. Rather surprisingly he was quite good about it, and told me that I would be offered an RAF officer to defend me in court. The bad news was that depending on the outcome, I might be charged by the RAF, because it might be considered that the name of the service had been brought into disrepute by my actions. Before I was dismissed, the SATCO smiled and said that would be the decision of the commanding officer, Wing Commander Scott.

Eventually the dreaded day in court arrived. Our defending officer turned out to be a young flight lieutenant from the general engineering flight. He was very sympathetic and after listening to our story he gave us a lecture about the 'follies of youth', but advised us to plead guilty. The atmosphere in court was very intimidating. The bench comprised of one man and two women, one of whom was the chairman; they whispered among themselves for quite a while, and when the chairman eventually got around to us she gave a long speech about young people taking liberties. She also mentioned that Margate tolerated serviceman only as far as they were expected to obey the letter of the law and set an example.

We were asked if we wished to speak up for ourselves, but our representative said that our written statements made it clear that we regretted what had happened and apologised to the court. He also apologised on behalf of the RAF and said that the service was considering punishing us for breaking the law. At that point Paddy gave me a sideways look that indicated he thought we were going to get it in the neck both ways, and be punished by the civil court and the RAF.

Our sentences were read out, and as Paddy was the main defendant his was first. He was fined £22 and given two endorsements on his driving license. The severity of the sentence made Paddy mutter some very bad language under his breath. Then it was my turn, and I was given a £12 fine and also received two endorsements for aiding and abetting. These were very harsh sentences considering that we barely earned £6 a week.

We had no money as such to pay the fines, and our defending officer had to make arrangements with the court for us to have the money deducted from our pay on a monthly basis. The only good thing that came out of it was that the CO decided that we would not be disciplined by the RAF as we had been punished enough. Shortly after our court appearance, Paddy was posted to Stornaway, and although I was later invited to his wedding in Northern Ireland, we were not to meet again for several years.

CHAPTER 9

Weather Matters

The evening of Friday 14 March 1969 began like many others and there was nothing to indicate that anything out of the ordinary might happen. When we went on duty at 5 p.m. the weather seemed to be set fair, and as there was a dance in the airmen's mess, I was looking forward to the arrival of the bus from Margate Sea Bathing Hospital carrying our guests, the nurses. Although I was on duty until 8 a.m. the following morning, I was hoping I would be able to sneak away for an hour or two to socialize with some of them.

At 5.30 p.m., half an hour after we had begun our watch, we received a 'Severe Weather Warning' from the meteorological office on the ground floor. I was the local controller's assistant that night, and when I got my copy of the warning I rang my friend Tim who was the Duty Meteorologist. Visibility was still quite good and we could clearly see Swingate Masts near Dover, which were 22 miles away. Jokingly, I told Tim he had got it all wrong and that he had better take more water with it in future. He laughed but assured me that his forecast was correct and that a blizzard was rapidly moving south towards us from East Anglia.

About an hour later, the approach controller received a call on the approach frequency from the pilot of a Vulcan who said that he was going to divert to us because the weather had closed his base in Lincolnshire down. The aircraft was low on fuel and it soon became clear that we were the only station still open in the south of England. With the weather rapidly closing in, that might not have been the case for much longer, and the pilot was cleared for a straight in approach. As usual there was a lot of flap and the powers that be discussed whether Manston had the necessary facilities;

the officers' mess was closed for the weekend and there was only a skeleton crew on at the Aircraft Servicing Flight.

Within a matter of minutes the sky began to darken and cloud over from the north-east; the wind began to get stronger, swinging from south to east. By the time the Vulcan was on final approach, the wind was gusting to 50 mph and the rain, which was fast turning to snow, was falling very heavily. The CO, Wing Commander Scott, and the SATCO were at odds as to where the Vulcan should be parked, but eventually they decided to put it on the ASP in front of the Britannia and the CL 44. Despite a strong crosswind that might have deterred many smaller aircraft, the Vulcan landed safely and the crew were brought to the control tower in the air traffic Land Rover 'Rover 1'.

The Vulcan's five-man crew consisted of the captain, co-pilot, navigator radar (bomb aimer), navigator plotter (navigator) and an air electronics officer (flight engineer). They were all very tired, but they were also very hungry, claiming that they had eaten all their in-flight rations hours ago. There were various discussions about where it would be best for them to be fed and in the meantime we supplied them with tea, coffee and biscuits.

Within a matter of minutes, a sudden emergency arose that required them to go back out immediately to attend to the aircraft. The wind was now gusting at over 70 mph and since the crew had parked the Vulcan it had swung around to the south. The Vulcan was parked facing straight into the wind and one of the ASF fitters, Bill Newman, had watched in horror as the nose wheel had lifted off the ground as the wind gusted ever stronger. The pilot asked for a towing arm to be taken out to move the aircraft around, but the only one that was suitable was locked away in the ground engineering flight hangar and nobody had the key!

There was no starter trolley either, and the crew faced the prospect of having to start up the engines on the internal batteries and then moving it under its own power. The two pilots were taken out in the air traffic Land Rover and climbed into the aircraft ready to start the engines. At the very last second, the ASF Land Rover arrived on the ASP, with the towing arm that had only been removed from the hangar after someone had smashed the door in. Within a few minutes it was connected and the Vulcan was very slowly turned out of the wind. With the pilots of the Vulcan back in the warm control tower, the subject of food came up again, and I was delegated by Corporal Turner as the airman to do a 'NAAFI run'.

Because I only had my battledress tunic to protect me from the snow and freezing cold wind, one of the crew, a young flying officer, kindly offered to lend me his flying suite. I welcomed the extra layer of clothing, but with all what was going on around us, I forgot to remove his badge of rank from the epaulets on the shoulder, a single thin black stripe. I thought nothing of it but as soon as I removed my battle dress tunic in the warmth of the NAAFI, a number of people started to joke about it. Bill Newman in particular began to mock me and made remarks about how easy it was for 'shinees' to get commissioned.

I ignored the banter and with pint in hand I went next door to the airmen's mess where Bill Reps the Head Cook told me I would have to wait to collect the sandwiches that had been ordered. Despite the very bad weather, some nurses had already arrived for the dance, including my girlfriend Susan, and so I took the opportunity to return to the NAAFI and have quick a pint. As I approached the bar again, I heard the dulcet tones of the station warrant officer, calling my name. As I addressed him, he inquired what I was doing wearing an officer's uniform, a flying officer who held the Queen's Commission? I explained to Flight Sergeant Goddard what had happened and said that I did not consider it constituted as 'uniform', so much as an extra layer of clothing.

The SWO told me not to be so cocky and that he could charge me for being improperly dressed. Despite repeatedly telling him that I had been loaned the flying suite to protect me from the extreme cold and bad weather, his demeanour remained the same. I had seen the SWO smiling occasionally and thought that he must have a dark sense of humour and that he must be joking. I was wrong!

The SWO pointed to the name on the left breast pocket that I had overlooked and asked who 'Flying Officer Johnson' was. I told him he was the officer who had loaned me the suite and if he wanted to check out my story he should ring air traffic control. At that point the SWO exploded and he asked in rather sarcastic way, 'Was I Leading Aircraftsman Bamford or Flying Officer Johnson?' He knew the answer to that of course, but then he demanded the name of the duty officer in air traffic control, because he was going to report me for being insolent.

I informed him that the duty air traffic control officer was Flight Lieutenant White, and the SWO said he would ring him immediately and report me for drinking on duty, as well as for being improperly dressed! With that the SWO left the building, muttering under his breath, and I decided to leave also, before I got into more trouble. I thought it typical that while Thanet was in the midst of one of the worst blizzards in living memory, the SWO was only interested in petty discipline. I collected the sandwiches from cook Bill Reps, and after bundling them together with a number of steak pies that I had bought in the NAAFI, I made my way back to the control tower.

By then the conditions outside were storm force and the blizzard was raging across the airfield; it was a 'white out'. As I crossed the main road near station headquarters, I could no longer see the lights in the control tower, and I held my head down as I struggled to walk against the strength of the wind. I presumed that I was heading in the right direction, but after several minutes had passed I realised that I was no nearer to the tower, and I looked up to discover that I had strayed onto the airfield. I did not know exactly where I was, but I knew I must be somewhere near the main Ramsgate road, or close to the grass runway. It was absolutely freezing cold and I suddenly became aware that in the blizzard I had become totally disorientated!

I continued struggling to plod through the snow and although I began to panic, my spirit was boosted when I saw the dim glow of a light in the distance that I knew must be coming from local control. Although I did not realise it at the time, I had actually crossed the main road that ran across the airfield and wandered several hundred yards to the south of the control tower. Had I continued on that course, I could have headed right across the airfield and into open countryside.

When I eventually arrived back in the tower covered in snow with icicles hanging off the end of my nose, I was greeted by Pete Turner with the words, 'Bamford ... where the bloody hell have you been? The officers are starving and I hope you didn't let those pies get cold.' I did not bother to try and explain what had happened and made light of my experience!

A little while later when things had quietened down and the crew of the Vulcan had retired to the officers' mess, Flight Lieutenant White asked to see me. As I walked into approach, I had a strange feeling that it was something to do with my brush with the SWO earlier in the evening. Sure enough, as I approached he smiled and greeted me with, 'Well, if it's not Flying Officer Bamford. Promotion comes quickly these days!'

Flight Lieutenant White then told me that the SWO had rung and he wanted me to be charged, but 'Chalky White', as he was known to everyone in the tower, said if I got him another cup of coffee he would forget all about it. It was an offer I could not refuse, and within a couple of minutes I was back in the approach room with the best cup of coffee that I ever made.

It was a very busy night and everyone stayed up to deal with ongoing work on the airfield and numerous calls from other airfields all over the

UK enquiring about our weather and serviceability. At one point there was even talk of the possibility that a number of civil airliners might divert to Manston, but that never happened and they probably went north to Prestwick. The 'snow blow' machine, an old Derwent jet engine, worked all night trying to clear the runway and western taxiway. The engine was fixed onto a mobile rig and the hot air from the blast melted snow and ice and dried the surfaces. It was a token effort, however, and as soon as the snow was cleared it was blown back onto the active again. Manston was effectively closed for the next 24 hours.

None of the nurses who had attended the station dance could get back to Margate because all the surrounding roads were blocked. My girlfriend spent the night in the sergeants' mess along with several of her friends, and I heard later they had a very good time being entertained by certain senior NCOs. Many other people were stranded that night, including the leader of the conservative party, Edward Heath. Mr Heath had attended a sailing club dinner and he was forced to spend the night at the Walpole Bay Hotel. Cars were abandoned all over Kent and altogether four people died, including one person who wandered onto a railway line and was hit by a train.

The next day was spent clearing up in the aftermath of the blizzard, and by lunchtime, Thanet District Council's snow-plough had eventually managed to clear the road across the airfield. One casualty was a car that belonged to Tim, the dentist who treated RAF personnel from his practice in Ramsgate. His white Ford Cortina was crushed by the snow plough and completely written-off. Fortunately, Tim was not in the car at the time; he was among several civilians who had taken refuge in the control tower and spent the night in Flight Planning. The Vulcan remained at Manston until Sunday when it took off with an ear-splitting roar that crackled the air for many miles around. By then the weather had turned fine again, and it was hard to believe that less than 48 hours earlier, Manston had been covered in snow and ice. It would not be the last time that I would witness such a scene.

A few months later in May, there was another memorable night caused by the weather. Three Canberras that were destined for Bassingbourne and the scrapman's torch arrived at Manston from Laarbruch in Germany. Because they landed later than scheduled, the aircraft had to remain at Manston overnight as Bassingbourne would have been closed by the time they got there. There was little fuss and the three crews were accommodated in the officers' mess. Arrangements were made for them to leave first thing the next morning.

I had drawn the 'short straw' as usual and was delegated to stay up all night on what promised to be another blustery evening. Just before midnight, I received a weather warning from the Met Office that forecast very strong winds during the early hours. When I took it upstairs and gave it to the local controller, Flight Sergeant Bob Kay, he said it might be a good idea if the Aircraft Servicing Flight went out and picketed the three Canberras to prevent them being damaged.

When I rang, ASF Bill Newman answered the phone and I got a rather short and rude reply: 'Have you seen the ★★★★★★★ weather out there? If you think we're going out in that, you can think again. Goodnight!' With that the line went dead. When I told Bob Kay about what had happened, he told me to make sure that it was recorded in the log book and to inform the duty ATCO, but other than that, he did not seem to be interested either. Eventually I settled down for the night; every hour when I received the weather I looked out of the window but I could see very little.

It was not until first light when I looked out of the SATCO's window and I saw that one the three Canberras seemed to have its nose raised in the air and was sitting at an odd angle. Then at about the same time, Bob Kay called on the squawk box to say he had seen it and to get ASF out straight away to check the damage. This time ASF did go out to the Canberras and reported back that one of them had been blown over on to its tail and its bomb doors and rear fuselage had been damaged. It was duly noted in the log book and we waited for the proverbial 'brown stuff' to hit the fan again.

It turned out that nobody cared very much about the Canberra being damaged and while the two other aircraft were flown out to Bassingbourne, WE168 remained at Manston. The aircraft sat on the pan for a number of weeks looking quite neglected until eventually Wing Commander Scott took an interest in it because he had flown the type many years before. He was keen to preserve it and prevent it from being burned by the Fire School (Central Training Establishment). In August it joined the Spitfire and Javelin outside SHQ and was put on display to the general public.

The irony is that WE168 remained on display at Manston until the events of 16 October 1987, when the south of England was hit by exceptionally strong winds. The Canberra was tipped back onto its tail again and damaged to such an extent that it had to be scrapped. It was strong winds that led to the Canberra becoming an exhibit at Manston, and it was strong winds that led up to its eventual demise!

A year or so later, another Canberra, WK124, a former 100 Squadron aircraft, was put on display to replace WE168. It had also been destined for

Canberra WK124 was RAF Manston's last Gate Guardian before the Spitfire and Hurricane Memorial Building (seen in the background) was opened in October 1988 by Dame Vera Lynn. Canberra WK124 replaced Canberra WE168, which was on display from 1969 until 1987. The aircraft was a B 2 converted TT 18, and it had served with 103, 59 and 213 Squadrons.

the scrap man's torch when it was commandeered to be put on the plinth previously occupied by WE168. However, a short while later, WK124 shared the same fate as its predecessor, and was dragged away to the CTE (Central Training Establishment) dump for training purposes.

CHAPTER 10

Putting My Foot in It

Easter 1969 was a busy time and there were a lot of British Midland flights; it had merged with Invicta a short while before in January and its Viscounts were carrying passengers to destinations all over Europe. British Midland had recently lost two Viscounts in accidents: G-AODG on 20 February at Castle Donnington, and G-AVJA at Manchester on 20 March. The first accident involved no fatalities but the aircraft was badly damaged, while at Manchester the two pilots were killed when the aircraft crashed taking-off on a training flight. Of the two stewardesses on board, one was killed, while the other, Miss Timson, managed to get clear and escaped from the rear cabin door that had been thrown open by the impact. Just a short while later I was to meet her and make a fool out of myself.

During my days off I often tried to get back home to Manchester and I sometimes travelled by train from Ramsgate to Victoria and then from Euston to Manchester Piccadilly. It could be an exhausting journey and I was always on the lookout for another way of getting there, possibly by having a lift or even a flight to Manchester. Invicta did sometimes fly into Manchester on positioning flights, but not very often from Manston. After the merger with British Midland I noticed that flights to Manchester became more regular, and I was keen that I should not miss out.

Every time I saw a movement on the board that was going to Manchester or Liverpool, I would ring Invicta Operations and ask if there was chance of me getting on it. When during a morning shift I saw that a British Midland Viscount was departing for Manchester on a positioning flight, I rang Bill Sheen, Invicta's operations officer. It was perfect timing; the aircraft was departing early afternoon and as I had been stood down that evening I did not even have to report to the tower for duty. Bill rang me back and said that as long as I signed a 'blood chitty' (indemnity form) the captain was willing to take me.

Within a couple of hours I was boarding the Viscount on the pan outside Invicta Operations; I found out that other than three good looking air hostesses, I was the only passenger. It was my dream come true! As soon as we got airborne, one of the girls gave me a cup of coffee. She sat next to me and asked me who I was and what I did at Manston. We struck up a conversation and very soon the other two girls sat behind us and the atmosphere was very convivial. I visited the flight deck and then returned to my seat and that is when everything went wrong!

As I sat down I started to chat about the recent air crash at Manchester involving another British Midland Viscount and asked if they had heard any news about what had happened? The atmosphere changed immediately and one of the girls got up and ran to the back of the aircraft, closely followed by her two colleagues. One of them returned some minutes later and told me that her colleague was Miss Timson, the sole survivor from the crash!

I felt rather stupid for even mentioning the accident, and the rest of the flight was made in silence. Just before we landed at Manchester, one of the girls came back to sit with me. She told me that it was her colleague's first flight since the crash, and that it was not my fault because I had no way of knowing that she was a survivor. However, I felt I had put my foot in it and ruined her comeback flight. Shortly after that the merger between Invicta and British Midland was broken up and the Viscounts became part of the British Midland fleet based at East Midlands Airport; there were no more opportunities to fly to Manchester from Manston.

It was about this time that I nearly caused a dreadful accident myself while acting as the approach controller's assistant. Uxbridge rang through to tell me that a Vulcan was about to enter the Low Lever Route at Entry Point 1 near Canterbury. The controller needed to know the time of the Vulcan's entry and of any conflicting traffic, but he was busy and every time I approached him he told me to just to wait a minute. Then my phone rang repeatedly with other stations asking for the weather and airfield state, and I forgot all about the clearance for the Vulcan.

Then the Vulcan suddenly appeared on the radar screen, just as a Canberra was also about to join the Low Level Route at Entry Point 1. The controller was aware of the Canberra but not of the Vulcan, and they were quite close to one another and only about a minute or so apart. Fortunately, the Vulcan had contacted Manston approach and the controller was able to warn the pilot about the Canberra. At the earliest opportunity when there was a quiet moment, the controller took me into the SATCO's office to give me a roasting.

He told me that my neglect of duty could have caused a serious accident, and had I not been a leading aircraftsman and technically, at least, still under training, I might have been put on a charge. He said he recognised that part of what had happened was his fault and he should have taken my message and not just told me to 'wait'. However, he said that in future if the controller was busy that I should pass any information on by writing it down on a piece of paper and passing it to him. As long as two captains of the aircraft involved did not make a report about the 'near miss' then he was willing to forget about it and not report it to the SATCO. If they did then it would be out of his hands and I would probably be charged! I was very fortunate because I never heard any more about it.

Over the Easter of 1969, Invicta and British Midland played a larger part in my life than the RAF did, and there were as many as a dozen movements a day at the peak. One evening, while carrying out an airfield inspection with one of the corporals on my shift, we noticed that a Viscount was sitting at the threshold of runway 29, about to take off. We watched as the pilots stopped the aircraft while they ran up its four Rolls-Royce Dart engines for a power check against the brakes.

The corporal reported to the tower on the Pye radio that all was well and then he turned to me and asked if I would like some 'fun' by trying to keep up with the aircraft as it ran down the runway. As he was driving I did not have much choice in the matter, and as the Viscount began to roll, our vehicle followed it down the runway. As the Viscount built up speed we began to get buffeted by the slipstream, but the corporal was determined to follow it as close as possible.

Just before the Viscount got airborne ahead of us, there was a sudden loud tearing noise and a sudden blast of cold air; the canvas roof of the Land Rover had been ripped off! As the aircraft climbed away, we slowly drove back to the tower with the roof hanging off and the vehicle looking very shabby as though it had been in a collision. The corporal dropped me off at the tower and then drove down to the MT section to see if he could get the Land Rover fixed before anyone inspected the Form 1629 and pinned him down to be responsible for the damage.

Despite the efforts of a few civilians in the MT section, the damage to the battered Land Rover could not be easily repaired and the corporal had to face the consequences. He made up a story about being hit by a sudden freak gust of wind out on the airfield but I do not think anyone believed him. Probably because he was something of a character, he did manage to get away without facing any disciplinary action, but needless to say he never made sergeant!

It was only much later when I accompanied the corporal on another trip across the airfield that I discovered why he always volunteered to do lighting inspections. He regularly 'liberated' cabbages, potatoes and other vegetables from the farmer's field at the end of runway 29, and he was doing a roaring trade in the married quarters. It was only when he was very nearly caught in the act by a farmer that his trade suddenly ceased.

CHAPTER 11

A Sad Loss

Before he was posted to Stornaway in Northern Island, I was assigned to work on a 'Blue Wind' exercise with Senior Aircraftsman Paddy Cochran, who was then a good friend. We were under the command of Flight Lieutenant Eric Winters, a member of the 'old school', and who could sometimes be a little difficult. The place where we were to work was the underground shelter beside the control tower, and as we soon discovered by the smell of the foul air, it had not been opened up for many years.

It was a bit different to working in the control tower and after we got a telephone line and squawk box connected, we began to get things organised; it was quite cosy down there, but a little bit damp. Most of the time there was only Paddy and me in the bunker and Flight Lieutenant Winters popped his head in occasionally, just to make sure we were plotting the figures we had been given onto the wall chart correctly. The exercise was to simulate that a nuclear warhead had exploded in the south-east, and our job was to work out in which direction the fall out was most likely to go and the areas most affected. In between that task we acted as a standby operations centre and logged all movements and information that was passed to us.

In early April I found myself working with Flight Lieutenant Winters again, as the local controller's assistant. I was supposed to have been the movements' clerk, but Corporal Peter Turner sent me upstairs because I had a very bad cold and was continually sneezing and coughing. Flight Lieutenant Winters also had a bad cold and so Peter thought it would be best to put us both together and keep the germs, especially the northern ones, in one place!

Some of the older controllers felt uncomfortable dealing with civil aircraft, probably because their crews followed different procedures than those flying military aircraft. After a while that afternoon, it became clear that Flight Lieutenant Winters was not coping very well with all the civil traffic. He especially seemed to be struggling with the issue of pilots having to wait for their airways' clearances. His R/T patter became irregular and he began to get irritable when pilots questioned his instructions from London ATCC.

To add to his misery and mine, the Chipmunks of Number 1 Air Experience Flight were very busy and constantly taking-off and landing. Some of them were using the main runway while a number of pilots chose to use the grass runway and it all got a bit hectic! At about 4 p.m., Flight Lieutenant Winters told the ATCO (Approach Controller) that he was not feeling well and he asked if he could be relieved by another controller. He told the warrant officer who took his place that all he needed was a good night's sleep but he would try and get an appointment with his doctor.

The following morning I felt particularly awful with an aching head and a very bad cough, I could quite happily have stayed in bed but I got up and reported for duty at 8 a.m. I went upstairs to local control but Flight Lieutenant Winters had not turned up for duty and the warrant officer said that he was going to Deal Hospital that morning to see a locum, because his own GP was on holiday in Malta. When he did eventually turn up at about 10 a.m. he looked awful and he spent some time that morning downstairs in approach drinking tea and coffee.

Normally Flight Lieutenant Winters was a stickler for dress codes and discipline, so much so that if an airman had a tie on he would insist that it had to be worn outside the jumper. If you undid more than one button on your tunic he would tell you to do it up or remove it, but then he would insist that you had to roll your shirt sleeves up to the regulation length.

However, during the previous afternoon and that morning, I unwittingly removed my tunic and he never said a word. In fact, during the quieter moments he got quite chatty and for the first time he began to talk about his personal life. He asked me where I came from and when I told him, he said he knew the area well because he came from Bolton. It was if he wanted to prove to me that he could be friendly. He told me something about his service career and the types of aircraft that he had flown and that originally he had been in the army.

It all seemed very surreal and as the morning slowly passed we were both looking forward to getting off duty at 12.30 p.m., but by then he looked very pale, tired and washed out. That evening I reported for duty at 5 p.m., but it was immediately recognised that I was in no fit condition to work. I was driven down to the medical centre where someone made the decision to admit me straight away.

I failed to remember much else for several days because I was delirious and regularly passing in and out of consciousness. A reoccurring dream was that I was flying in a Canberra and struggling with the controls to keep it in the air. I had never flown in a Canberra although I had seen many of them as they passed through Manston; I can only think it was the subconscious playing tricks!

For several more days I continued to drift in and out of consciousness, unaware of my surroundings, but gradually I began to recover. As I had a history of bronchitis from early childhood, the medical centre would not release me without being checked out by a doctor, but he eventually discharged and told me to rest.

I was released from the medical centre on the evening of Friday 11 April and the first place that I went was to the NAAFI to see if anyone that I knew was about. There were not many people in the bar and I asked the manager, Charlie, what everybody had been up to during my absence? The first thing he said in his gloomy northern accent was, 'It's a bad do about Flight Lieutenant Winters. You were very lucky'. When I asked what he meant, Charlie told me that he had just heard that he had died earlier that day in Ramsgate Hospital. I still do not know why, but the news brought me close to tears. The tragic death of an officer I barely knew really touched my emotions.

At the beginning of the following week I went back to work, although I still did not feel like my health was anything like back to normal. I was more than surprised when I heard that I was to be on duty to attend Flight Lieutenant Winters' Funeral Parade. Not that I objected in principal, but having been so close to him during the final shift in the control tower and having been quite ill myself, I thought I might have been excused.

The parade was held on 18 April in the afternoon; it was a particularly sombre occasion, and one that I think everyone felt uncomfortable with. He had served with distinction during the war, and having transferred to the RAF from the Royal Artillery in December 1940, he had flown Spitfires, Wellingtons, Liberators and Yorks. He had been awarded the DFC in August 1945. A few of us felt that he deserved better and perhaps the funeral parade should have been held at Cranwell or Uxbridge. RAF Manston was a pleasant enough place to be, and it had strong traditions and a long history, but with barely 100 airmen and officers, the station was not big enough to provide the dignified ceremony that such an occasion deserved.

The funeral parade consisted of twenty airmen under the orders of the SWO Flight Sergeant Brian Goddard. They wore Number 1 Dress. The parade was lined up along the road that ran from SHQ, past the sergeants' mess and airmen's mess, to the western end of the station. The procession included the hearse that flew the RAF ensign, and another couple of cars carrying the family, followed by Wing Commander Scott's Austin 1800. As it drove past, there was a fly past by the Chipmunks from Number 1 Air Experience Flight; it was quite fitting as until recently, Flight Lieutenant Winters had still flown with the unit, and the humble single-engine training aircraft was the last type that he ever flew.

Flight Lieutenant Eric Winters' wife and three children attended the funeral at RAF Manston; his body was then taken back to Bolton for another final service before being cremated. The cause of death was given as Bronco Pneumonia (Post Influenza). He was just fifty years old and it seemed ironic to me that a man who had seen so much action – in the Berlin Airlift and the 'Mau Mau' uprising in Kenya – should die of what was basically a very bad cold! Despite the fact that Flight Lieutenant Winters was something of a disciplinarian and often pedantic, I have always remembered fondly those final hours with him in the control tower.

CHAPTER 12

The US Connection

May 1969 was also a memorable month because of a particularly rare and strange incident involving the theft of an American C 130 Hercules from RAF Mildenhall in Suffolk. In the early hours of 23 May I was sleeping in the monitor's room, and just after 5 a.m., I heard voices repeatedly calling on some of the frequencies that had been left switched on.

The monitor's room was adjacent to the movements room, and it was only separated by a glass-panelled door that was normally left open during the day. In all the time that I was at Manston, the monitor's room was never used for its original purpose, but was just a place where things were stored or where people on night shift slept when the opportunity arose.

The voices over the R/T seemed very distant, but when I woke up I could hear there was a lot of chatter on the military emergency frequency of 243.00 and the NATO common approach frequency of 122.1. When a frequency was in use, a light came on above the designated transmit/receive switch. Although it was common for the signal to be too weak for us to hear what was being said, we could always tell if a channel was in use because the light indicated that someone was transmitting.

As I struggled to my feet with my eyes full of sleep, I could see that there was already some activity in the movements room and I was soon asked to make a brew and get the weather information up on the boards in approach. Nobody was sure what was happening, but there were rumours that an aircraft was in trouble and that the pilot might be diverting to Manston. Then slowly, piece by piece, information gradually came in that a Lockheed Hercules transport aircraft from the 316th Tactical Airlift Wing at Mildenhall had been stolen by a disgruntled crew chief.

It all seemed a bit bizarre when we heard later that a number of fighters, probably F 100 Super Sabres from Bentwaters, had taken off in pursuit. It was the pilots of those aircraft that I had heard over the radio, calling blind and trying to make contact. The chatter went on for several hours as they tried to get the offending airman to respond. As he was below the height where he might get picked up by radar, they were probably uncertain of his position, and were trying to lure him into making contact. It seems highly unlikely that they were actually trying to persuade him to return to Mildenhall because of the risks posed by an inexperienced pilot at the controls of a large four-engine transport aircraft.

A fully-laden Hercules weighs approximately 60 tons, but despite its weight and size it is a very versatile aircraft, capable even of landing on the deck of an aircraft carrier. The US Navy conducted trials and a single KC-130F made twenty-one landings and twenty-nine 'touch and gos' on the deck of USS *Forrestal* without the use of a hook. However, those landings were carried out in perfect conditions with an experienced crew at the controls. The pilot at the controls of the Hercules stolen from Mildenhall had no experience of flying the aircraft, and presented a hazard to other aircraft and to people on the ground.

At Manston, the duty controller was kept busy talking to both civilian and military controllers at London Centre and Uxbridge, receiving information and giving them updates. We were told that the aircraft was flying in the area of the English Channel, where he might try to abandon it; all eyes were on the 787 search radar looking for any unusual trace.

We heard that the pilot, later identified as Sergeant Paul Myers, did have some limited flying experience, but he had only flown light aircraft such as Cessnas. His role as crew chief at Mildenhall had authorised him to start the engines, run them up to test them, and then, if required, to taxi the aircraft. That is how he had managed to get away from Mildenhall; after feigning a taxi test to the runway threshold, he had applied full power and taken off.

For several hours the chat over the R/T continued, but any hope that the airman might get in touch seemed to fade with each hour. When we went off watch at 8 a.m., things had quietened down, and rumours were already beginning to spread that the Hercules had been shot down by American fighters. The only evidence that we had was a single contact that the approach controllers saw on the 787 search radar. They suspected that this was the Hercules being 'shadowed' by a number of other unidentified contacts (Angels), which may or may not have been the American fighters. None of the aircraft on the screen were displaying any IFF (Identification

Friend or Foe) which seemed rather unusual, and their origins were unknown.

At about 8.30 a.m. the calls and challenges over the R/T stopped, and everything suddenly went very quiet. It seemed like the scenario had ended one way or another, but the Americans did not release any information to confirm what had happened. It is now known that the Hercules crashed off Alderney in the Channel Islands, but the question remains whether the pilot lost control or whether he was shot down.

It is highly unlikely that information will ever be released as to the ultimate fate of Sergeant Myers and the stolen Hercules, but many of those American servicemen who were at Mildenhall at the time think that the aircraft was shot down. The suggestion is that F 100s Super Sabres from Lakenheath, though temporarily based at Mildenhall, shot it down to prevent it crashing in a built-up area in nearby France. One airman even claims to have seen photos of the wreckage 'riddled with bullet holes', but that is just hearsay.

The factors leading up to the incident are open to speculation, but it has been suggested that Sergeant Myers was upset that his tour of duty had been extended for a second time, and that he was unable to return home to see his wife and child. It has been claimed that he was drinking heavily in the hours that led up to him stealing the plane, and that he had told some of his fellow senior NCOs what he intended to do. Nobody took any notice of him, and the theft put into action a series of events that ended in tragedy.

A short while after that incident there was another exciting episode at Manston involving a US Navy Hercules, which arrived unannounced, just before mid-day one bright and sunny morning. I was acting as the approach controller's assistant and the first we knew of it was when a voice with a deep American drawl called 'Manston this Hotel Lima 12 inbound from Dover flight level five zero'. The controller immediately looked up at the movement's board and accused me of not telling him about it and failing to write it up on the board. I quickly checked with Movements next door and found that they had no record of the flight. Nobody else had any information on it either, except London Airways who had only heard of the flight after it had called them on entering controlled airspace!

Within a matter of minutes, the silver and white Hercules was rolling down the runway; its arrival took everyone by surprise. The SATCO went up to local control immediately and decided that it should be parked on the ASP by the control tower, which was the usual place for foreign visitors. When ASF was informed about the Hercules they got a bit stroppy and the

A Lockheed P.3 Orion reconnaissance of the US Navy at Manston. American aircraft were regular visitors, but technical and security problems always seemed to cloud their presence. (*Mr D.A. Wilks*)

warrant officer said that as they had not previously been informed about it, the aircraft's crew would have to wait until they were ready. Meanwhile, the crew of the Hercules were also being less than helpful, and the pilots refused to tell the local controller about their departure airfield, their intentions and destination, and whether the aircraft required re-fuelling.

The crew's reluctance to communicate was not very helpful, but when the ASF Land-Rover finally arrived at the aircraft, the situation came to a head. Bill and Rod were approached and threatened by armed guards who were very belligerent and demanded that they 'Back off' and make no attempt to board the aircraft. Not surprisingly, a stand-off developed, with the ASF boldly reminding the aircraft guards that Manston was an RAF airfield, not a '★★★★★★★' American base. It all got rather nasty and within a short while both the warrant officer from ASF and Wing Commander Scott arrived at the aircraft to try to sort things out.

ASF eventually withdrew its men from around the aircraft and refused to service the Hercules while they were surrounded by armed guards;

meanwhile the Hercules' crew maintained their refusal to co-operate. For fifteen or twenty minutes there was a stand-off, but then all of a sudden, unannounced, HL12 started its engines again. With minimal communication between the control tower and pilots, the Hercules taxied out for runway 29. Its crew were in so much of a hurry that the fire section did not have time to close the barriers on the main road and at least one motorist had a close encounter when the Hercules lumbered across in front of him. They had not filed a flight plan, and much to the annoyance of London ATCC, the aircraft joined airways at Dover without a clearance and disappeared off the radar screens, last seen heading south.

The whole episode remained a mystery, but rumours later abounded that the Hercules belonged to a US Naval unit, VR24, which was based in Spain at La Rota. The unit had previously been based at West Malling, not a great distance from Manston. It was suggested the pilot had landed at Manston in error, but whether that was the case we never found out.

CHAPTER 13

Stuck in the Mud

The number of civil aircraft arriving at Manston increased dramatically during 1969 and Air Spain and Loftleider, the Icelandic airline, were regular visitors. Air Spain had purchased a number of British Eagle's Britannias, previously registered G-AOVR, G-AOVE and G-ARWZ. Now emblazoned in the new white, blue and orange colours of Air Spain, the aircraft had been re-registered EC-BFJ, EC-BFK and EC-BFL.

The introduction of these cargo flights that mainly carried fruit from Spain was not without its problems; Manston's narrow taxiways were not big enough for the modern generation of airliners such as the Britannia and Boeing 707. The first time an Air Spain Britannia arrived it was parked on the central taxiway, but its pilots could not negotiate the turnings with the nose wheel steering. Its nose wheel ran on to the grass and dug into the soft earth, so deep that even with full power on, all four engines could not move it.

This was another occasion when the SATCO and station commander were called out in the middle of the night to supervise the recovery of a foreign aircraft that was being handled by Invicta. As usual, Invicta got the blame for the fiasco, and it was claimed that the aircraft marshaller had been unaware the Britannia would be unable to turn in an area where Vicounts and DC 4s manoeuvred regularly. The Aircraft Servicing Flight were on the scene straight away, but as had happened earlier in the year with the Vulcan, the crew did not have a tow bar for a Britannia, and all they could do was to suggest unloading it where it sat!

That is what happened and 18 tons of ripe tomatoes from Tenerife were slowly off-loaded in a laborious process that involved rollers having to be put in place so that the cardboard boxes could be sent down into the back of waiting lorries. While that was being done the nose wheel was being dug out, with metal planking and wire being placed around the tyres and under the wheels so that they would gain more traction. It was first light by the time the aircraft had been emptied and everyone stood by to see if it could move out off the boggy ground under its own power. It took several attempts and only by the Britannia's pilots putting the propellers into reverse thrust did the aircraft finally move and release its nose wheel.

Very cautiously and under strict guidance of an aircraft marshaller, the pilots turned the aircraft around and arrived at the runway threshold to take off. They must have been happy to see the back of Manston after their night-long experience. Air Spain Britannias continued to visit, but I think that particular crew might not have been flying them. After this incident, steel planking was used regularly to reinforce all the corners on the eastern and northern taxiways, but that didn't prevent other incidents from occurring through a lack of knowledge and understanding.

One evening we got a flight plan to confirm that a CL 44 would be arriving in the early hours of the morning from Tenerife; nothing unusual in itself. What was different was the registration of the aircraft, TF-LLJ, which I immediately identified as a CL 44J. Originally known as the Canadair 400 (also Rolls-Royce 400), the CL 44J was a larger, longer version of the CL 44D – in fact 15 feet 2 inches longer – and it could carry up to 189 passengers. At the time it was the aircraft that could carry the greatest number of passengers across the trans-Atlantic routes, more than either the Boeing 707 or the DC 8. Measured from the nose wheel to the main undercarriage, it had a very long wheel base, and I was sure that it would present some difficulties in negotiating Manston's taxiways.

It was about 7 p.m. when I took the local controller a cup of coffee; as it happened, the SATCO was up in local control, showing round a group from the Wives' Club. I thought it was a good time to redeem myself and get into his good books. Choosing my moment carefully, I approached him.

'Excuse me, sir, can I have quick word?'

He looked a bit taken aback at my intrusion but said, 'Yes Bamford … what is it?'

I began to explain, 'We have a CL 44 due in later on tonight, sir, and I think there could be problems with it – it's a CL 44J.'

The SATCO looked puzzled and said to the local controller, 'Nothing odd about that is there flight?'

The controller was put on the spot and answered, 'No sir ... we've had one parked on the ASP for months.'

I tried to explain the difference between the aircraft sitting on the ASP and the larger CL 44J, but it was obvious that I was wasting my time. The SATCO did not want to listen and he told me to go downstairs and make a brew for his female guests who were happily cackling away among themselves. Ten minutes later, when I returned with a tray full of tea and coffee, I tried to talk to him again but he totally ignored me and continued to demonstrate to the women how the airfield lighting panel worked. I never said any more about it, and decided to see what would happen at 4 a.m. when the aircraft landed!

In the early hours of the morning I thought I had better warn Invicta Airways about the impending problem, and when Operations rang to give me details of an unscheduled outbound flight, I told Bill about my concerns. Ignorance was bliss and I might have been talking to the 'Man on the Moon' for the good it did; he was not in the least bit interested. A short time later, the CL 44 called approach and began its descent off airways into Manston. I gave Invicta the usual 10-minute call and asked the operations officer where the plane was to be parked. They said to park it up on the pans outside their operations building, but as it turned out the CL 44 never got that far; my prediction proved to be correct.

The aircraft approached over Acol, and after landing on runway 11, its pilot was given instructions about where to turn off and the directions across the northern and central taxiways. Suddenly, as with the Air Spain Britannia a few weeks before, the R/T went very quiet as the pilots pondered over their situation. And then came the cry for help.

'Manston ... Loftleider Lima Juliet ... we have a problem ... we cannot make the turn off the runway.'

The pilot was told to maintain his position and wait for help to arrive, but when he shut down the engines it was obvious that this was going to be another long night!

Within a few minutes, a number of vehicles had arrived on the scene, including Crash 1, the ASF Land-Rover and a marshaller from Invicta. There was some confusion about whose responsibility it was to sort the problem out, and although Invicta were handling the aircraft, the ASF duty crew were aware that they had a part to play in resolving the problem. As it happened, it soon became clear to both parties that the aircraft was well and truly stuck, and it was not going to be able to get off the runway onto the taxiway. The marshaller plugged a lead into the aircraft's intercom system and spoke to the pilot who made it clear that he was not going any further and the aircraft would have to be unloaded where it was!

It was another early morning call for Wing Commander Scott and the SATCO, who arrived in the control tower to sort out the mess. This was even worse than the previous incident with the Air Spain Britannia, because this time the runway was completely blocked. I was asked to send a NOTAM (Notice for Airman) to Uxbridge which stated that the airfield was closed until further notice; for a Master Diversion Airfield that was not a good thing to happen. It was not long before the controller at Uxbridge rang up and wanted to know what was going on. We thought it only right that he should be put through to our SATCO and let him explain. The SATCO picked up the telephone, and he had a few awkward moments of explaining to do.

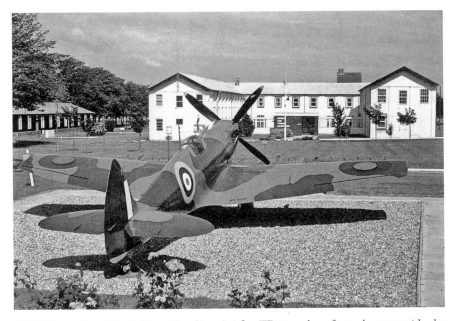

RAF Manston's original Gate Guardian, Spitfire TB572, taken from the rear with the Station Headquarters building in the background, 1974. The Spitfire was removed from Manston in July 1978 to be restored by the Medway Branch of the Royal Aeronautical Society. It was returned in September 1979 in time for the Battle of Britain day. After that it was kept under cover in a hangar until June 1981 when it was moved into the Spitfire Memorial Building, opened by Air Vice-Marshal J. F. G. Howe CBE, AFC on 13 June 1981. Subsequently, in October 1988, Hurricane LF751 was moved to compliment the Spitfire and the museum became 'The Spitfire and Hurricane Memorial Building'. (*John Williams*)

The aircraft remained on the runway threshold for several hours, but when it had been unloaded, the pilot started the engines; being 20 tons lighter, he managed to turn on the main runway. After taxiing back to the threshold of runway 11, the aircraft finally took off and the airfield opened for business again. By that time, Manston had been closed for over 4 hours, and had an emergency occurred it could have had major consequences; all because the SATCO would not listen!

When the annual NATO Tiger Meet was held in August 1969, a variety of interesting foreign aircraft, including a number of Fiat G 91s from the Luftwaffe's Jabo 431 passed through Manston. The meeting that year was hosted by the USAAF 79th Fighter Squadron at Woodbridge, and among the RAF contingent were the Lightnings of 74 Squadron. The Italian Air Force also visited Manston with its Fiat G 91s and a rare DC 6 that provided support and maintenance for the aircraft.

During this period there was certainly never a dull moment and we never knew what was going to turn up next in the array of new and foreign types of aircraft. Among them were the Fouga Magisters of both the French and Belgian air forces. The two-seat trainer that had been designed by the French in the '50s had a novel 'V'-shaped tailplane instead of the traditional fin. As they parked up on the ASP by the control tower, it was easy to walk over to them and have a look around.

Most of the German, French and Belgian pilots spoke good English, and unlike the Americans they were always willing to let us inspect their aircraft. Many of them, particularly the Germans, had heard about Manston's reputation as a Battle of Britain station, and they were keen to have a look around the station's Gate Guardian, Spitfire TB572, parked in front of SHQ. Thirty years after the Battle of Britain, the Spitfire and RAF Manston evoked powerful emotions.

CHAPTER 14

Marriage and Friendship

Over the Easter of 1969, my parents visited Thanet for the first time after I had announced that my girlfriend Susan and I were getting engaged. Things had happened a bit fast even by my standards and they were travelling to meet Susan's parents and the rest of her family who lived in Ramsgate. They travelled down from Manchester to London on the overnight bus on a Friday night, and then caught the train from Victoria to Ramsgate. They stayed over the weekend of 5 April at a boarding house in Broadstairs, the owner being a friend of Hughie O'Neil, the most senior aircraftsman on my shift.

It felt strange to have my mother and father around again, but the weekend went well, and the usual pleasantries were exchanged. Both sets of parents went along with the pretence that we would soon be 'married and live happily ever after', but in my heart I knew it was not going to happen. Just a short time later, Susan told me that she had met up with her old boyfriend and she was calling the engagement off. We were walking around Margate Harbour at the time, and to begin with I just wanted to throw myself in the water. But within a short time I got over it, and I met someone else.

A few months later I was invited to my friend Paddy's wedding in Northern Ireland; he had recently been posted up to Stornaway to work at a signals unit, whose role was confidential. I had not seen much of Paddy for quite a while, but even before his departure our friendship had begun to deteriorate and I was starting to get bored with his quirky ways. Despite the fact that he claimed to miss his fiancée in Northern Ireland, he was more than happy to continue seeing various women, including a couple of nurses who worked at the sea bathing hospital. After splitting up with my girlfriend Susan in April, I had begun to mix with a different crowd made up mainly of some of the new lads who had recently been posted in.

Despite our differences of opinion, Paddy and I had had some good times together, and female company was never hard to find when he had been around. One of the most memorable occasions was one night when we were in the Balhi Hia Bar on the seafront in Margate and the comedian Marty Feldman walked in. With his strange eyes he was unmistakable, and although he said very little, he bought everyone drinks and stayed in the bar for quite a while. It turned out that he was filming a sketch in Margate's Dreamland Amusement Park, which is still seen on television to this day. It was a night to remember and thanks to the bar manager Dave, everyone got very drunk!

I was pleased to be invited to Paddy's long-proposed wedding, but in 1969, Northern Ireland was not a good place for a British serviceman to be. However, I put away my bad feelings and decided to risk it; I booked my passage to travel to Belfast by train from London, and ferry from Stranraer to Larne.

When I arrived at Euston Station to catch my train to Stranraer, I observed that the Evening Standard billboards were headlining the troubles in Northern Ireland, with bombs going off and people rioting. It was just a few days after Operation Banner had begun on 15 August 1969, and British troops had been sent into Northern Ireland for the first time in many years. Little did anyone suspect then that the operation would continue for thirty-eight years, and that it would cost the lives of hundreds of innocent people.

I was in two minds whether to continue my journey to Northern Ireland, but I thought that I could not let Paddy down because in his letter he had suggested that in the absence of his brother, I might be the Best Man. Just to add to my troubles, I had made the mistake of travelling to London in uniform, which would have made me an obvious target on the other side of the water. To make myself less conspicuous, once I had boarded the train I changed into civvies in the toilet, and then began drinking with a couple of uniformed squaddies who were in a jovial mood.

Within a short while a number of other servicemen joined our group, and we ended up occupying the best part of half a carriage. The conversation was all about Northern Ireland, and most of the army lads thought that they would be going there very soon. The general opinion was that it was a dangerous place, and when I told them that was where I was going, they told me that I must be mad!

I was informed that I would be marked out as a serviceman immediately by my short haircut, style of dress and the fact that I was carrying a blue RAF-issue holdall. When I told them that my friend was from Londonderry and would look after me, they laughed and said that he would be lucky if he could look after himself. Their banter cast doubts in my mind because I did not even know how to find my way to Paddy's house on the Creggan Estate in Londonderry; suddenly I began to feel very vulnerable! As the train carried me further north my doubts increased, and when it stopped at Crewe to change the electric engine for a diesel, I knew I had to decide what to do.

Of my friends from the army who remained on the train, some were goading me into abandoning my trip to Northern Ireland, while a few others said that I should take the risk and go. Having had so many cans of beer, things were a bit hazy, and I stepped down from the train to get some fresh air so that I could think more clearly. Then there was a sudden shrill blast on a whistle and the guard started waving his flag and shouting to close the door; I only had seconds to make a decision.

Subconsciously, I had already made it, and so I leapt back into the carriage, grabbed my holdall off the rack and shouted goodbye to my travelling companions. It was only when the train had disappeared into the night that I realised I had left behind the quilt that was to have been my wedding present. There was nothing I could do about it, but I felt relieved that I would be spending the night at home in Manchester, rather than on board a ship on the Stranrear to Larne crossing.

Because it was so late, my choices for trains were very limited. I chose a slow train to Macclesfield, and after stopping at every station on the line, I eventually caught a connection and arrived at Manchester Piccadilly after midnight. I got a taxi to my home in Pendlebury, and after several minutes of shouting through the letterbox, my mother let me in and I was soon in bed, dreaming of being shot at in Northern Ireland.

I decided to spend a few days of my leave in Manchester, but my mother was unable to understand why I had abandoned my journey to Northern Ireland. She had met Paddy briefly some months before when he had accompanied me home on a few days off; she thought he was a lovely lad and that I had let him down badly. I did not want to spoil her opinion of him so I kept quiet about recent events. I soon got bored and returned to Manston, where I now felt more at home than in Manchester.

I never regretted my decision not to attend Paddy's wedding, especially after hearing about the bombings, shootings and killings that were happening during that period. Paddy did send me a stinking letter some time later, telling me exactly what he thought of me, but I ignored it, and I had no further contact with him for another three years, when my time in the RAF had come to an end.

CHAPTER 15

Out and About

In July I applied for an overseas posting and I was put on the Pre-Warning Roster (PWR) almost immediately, which meant I could have been posted anywhere in the world at short notice. I had applied to be posted to either Hong Kong or Gan, the latter being a small island in the Indian Ocean that was used by the RAF as a staging post to the Far East. The reality was that I just wanted to serve overseas, and with the exception of Germany, I was not bothered where they sent me.

Things happened very quickly, and at the beginning of August I got a telephone call from Bill Williams in the general office. Bill might have been a civilian, but with the exception of Squadron Leader White, he was probably the most important person on the station. He ran the general office and wielded a great deal of influence in every department. Although he did not directly control postings, he probably had a lot of say on who went where. Bill told me that my application for a posting had been accepted, but as I did not have a current passport, and I would need to get one right away.

In the general office I filled in the passport application and many other forms and soon Bill told me that he had made an appointment for me to have some photographs taken. Almost immediately I was dispatched to a photographer's in Margate, and within a matter of days I received my first proper passport. It stated my profession as 'Government Service', which I joked about, telling people that I was a 'secret agent'. Unwittingly, immigration clerks in certain Middle East countries actually thought that I was a secret agent, and over the years the passport was to get me into quite a bit of trouble!

Many months went by and I never heard a thing about my application for an overseas posting to Gan or anywhere else. Some of those I worked with such as Pete Abel and Hughie O'Neil used to tease me by telling me that it was quite likely I would spend the whole of my service life at Manston. I pondered on that prospect for many hours, but I realised that there were far worse places I could be. Some of the recent arrivals like Brian from Stoke, Dave from Reading and Jim from the West Country, proved to be good friends and began to liven up what was often a dull and boring station.

Brian and Dave were both electricians who often mocked each other's ability to do such simple things as recharge the battery on a glim lamp. Jim − not his real name, but a nickname because his surname was Reeves − was also very amusing, and he worked on the General Engineering Flight. Another member of our group was Jack, but he was older than us and had a bald head which was often the source of some amusement.

After a while we all got fed up with the delights of Margate and Ramsgate, and so we began to visit the public houses in the village of Minster, about a mile beyond the airfield. The outskirts of Minster were just a short distance from the airfield boundary across the Canterbury Road, but it was quite difficult to get there by public transport. Brian and Dave came up with the idea of walking to Minster across the airfield, by going up the western taxiway and cutting across the main runway near the threshold of runway 11.

Trespassing on the airfield without authorisation was a risky business, and if we had been caught we would have been in deep trouble, both with our section commanders and with the CO. Our trips had to be timed to perfection so that we would avoid being spotted by someone from air traffic carrying out an airfield inspection or going out to the runway caravan. In fact, we also had to avoid the duty runway controller when he was on duty in the caravan at the end of the runway. Some shift corporals preferred to be out there rather than in the control tower, even if there were no movements and their presence meant that we had to take a long diversion.

Having successfully crossed the airfield, we usually stopped off at the Prospect Inn (now the Holiday Express Inn) for a pint of beer or glass or Mead, before we walked down the road into the village. Our main haunts were the Sadler's Arms and the New Inn, because the other pub in the village, the Bell, was considered to be a bit exclusive. Two brothers who had the grass-cutting and maintenance contracts at Manston were regulars at the Sadler's and they used to tease us endlessly, calling us the 'the young boys in blue' and other names which are not fit for print.

They worked as contractors for what was then the Ministry of Public Works, and so in return we used to tell them that they were just slaves of the 'Ministry of Public Blunders and Wonders'. When that name was changed to the Department of the Environment, we told them that they were just navvies of the 'Department of Excuses'. It was all good-natured ribaldry and we all got on very well with the local community.

Sometimes we would just walk across the airfield and visit the Jolly Farmer in the village where there was always a pleasant welcome from the host and hostess, Bert and Ena Turner. Bert was something of a legend in football circles because in the 1946 FA Cup Final, he became the first player to score a goal for both sides.

Bert was playing for Charlton Athletic against Derby County and the game was goalless until the 85th minute when he managed to put the ball into his own net. A minute later, Bert took a free kick and made up for his mistake by scoring the equaliser. The record of a player scoring for both sides was to stand until 1981 when Tommy Hutchinson of Manchester City also scored an own goal and then another for his team against Tottenham. As a result of Bert's late goal the 1946 Cup Final went into extra time, but Derby scored three more goals and the final score was Charlton 1 Derby 4.

Bert's wife, Ena, always called us 'Her Boys', and although there is no doubt that she thought most highly of anyone who served in the RAF, she stood no nonsense. On one occasion we returned to the JF for last orders having spent most of the night in Margate. I had brought along a red obstruction light off some road works and when Ena saw the lamp, she refused to serve me again until I took it back to where I had got it from. The next day I had to get a friend to drive me into Margate, return the lamp and then go with me to the JF to confirm what I had done. She drove a hard bargain!

Ena always had a special soft spot for officers and aircrew. Subsequently, the lounge bar was called the 'Cockpit Bar', and was reserved exclusively for them. We airmen, the 'Erks', were not allowed on that side of the pub, but that did not really make much difference to us as a pint of beer was two pence cheaper (old money) in the public bar.

There was always a bit of hustle going on in the Jolly Farmer, and many of those who frequented it were the staff and aircrew from Invicta Airlines, who used the place so often that it became known as 'Base Operations'. Unsurprisingly, it was a den of rumours concerning all aspects of civil and military aviation. One of the first rumours I remember was Bert's claim that Invicta was going to re-equip its fleet with Boeing 707s. It was based upon the fact that someone had painted a Boeing 707 in Invicta colours and given the picture to Ena. The rumour was not entirely wrong, but it was a little premature because it was not until 1971 that Invicta purchased a former American Airlines Boeing 720, N7528A. It arrived at Manston for the first time on 3 November 1971 in an overall white colour scheme, to be repainted in Invicta's colours. It was given the British registration of G-BCBA, but it had little impact on Invicta's operations and mainly operated out of East Midland's Airport. Invicta only owned the Boeing for a short while, and it was sold by its owners, European Ferries, in May 1974.

In Ramsgate, the Walmer Castle on Addington Street became one of our favourite watering holes, but it was only a small pub where everyone squeezed in together. Danny, the landlord, was a very hospitable Irishman who loved playing darts, and it was not long before he enticed us into playing for the pub team. The pub was also frequented by a number of other people that we knew, including Tim, the dentist, who I had met on my very

Former American Airlines Boeing 720. Despite rumours that Invicta had purchased a 'Boeing' back in 1970 when a painting of it appeared on the wall of the Jolly Farmer pub, it did not arrive at Manston until November 1973. It was registered G-BCBA but it saw little service with Invicta and was sold in 1975. (*Mr D. A. Wilks*)

first day at Manston, and old Bert, who worked on the PBX exchange on the base.

Bert was one of life's characters but he was also a first-class scrounger. Often when we met him he would claim to have some rare bit of information about what was to going to happen at Manston, and if we bought him a drink he would tell us about it. We always bought him a drink because we felt sorry for him, but his bits of information always proved to be something that we already knew or had recently appeared on station standing orders. There was something of a lovable roguish quality about Bert that we all liked, and being an 'old soldier', we felt obliged to talk to him and buy him drinks.

One thing that puzzled us for quite a while about the Walmer Castle was that a group of young women regularly appeared in the pub, but hardly ever bought a drink. If they did buy a drink it was normally no more than a half of beer that lasted them all evening. They tended to wander in and out of the pub at regular intervals, and were always adjusting their make-up, powdering their noses and putting on lipstick. Danny had regularly pointed out that he was not running a 'charity', but he was very coy when we asked about the women. The mystery was only solved when we saw a couple of the women down in the harbour boarding a ship with a couple of very rough looking sailors – they were prostitutes!

In those days, ships that delivered Volkswagen cars from Hamburg used to be moored in the inner basin of Ramsgate harbour. They were quite big vessels and only just fitted through the outer lock gates to be moored against the harbour wall. The pub was only a short distance from the harbour and all the girls had to do was cross the road, descend a series of steps known as 'Jacob's Ladder', and they were almost by the side of the ship. We could not believe how naïve we had been and soon afterwards we got the impression that the girls had discovered that we knew their 'secret'. Some nights there was a lot of giggling with them pointing towards our table and it made us all a little uncomfortable. We thought we knew all about women up to that point, but the fact we had been mixing with a bunch of prostitutes for several months without knowing it surprised us all!

Some time later, while we were in the pub, our friend Jack complained that he had found a nasty rash around his nether regions, and Brian shouted out scornfully, 'He's got the clap!'

'No I haven't' said Jack defensively, 'I haven't been with a woman for ages.'

'I'm not surprised', said Brian, 'you're too bloody ugly. But I bet you've been off with one of them bints over there!'

Jack denied any such thing and the matter was only resolved when he visited the medical officer a few days later, but the diagnosis was not what he expected.

'What kind of washing powder do you use to wash your underwear,' asked the doctor, 'presuming, of course, that you do wash it?'

'Of course I do,' said Jack, 'I use one of the new biological washing type powders. Why?'

'Because you have nappy rash,' declared the doctor. 'Congratulations!'

The news spread around the camp very quickly, and everyone found the fact that an airman in his thirties had nappy rash very amusing.

The only night club in Ramsgate at that time was Neros, which was situated on the seafront near Merry England, the original Ramsgate railway station. In 1969, another club called the 'Tiberius' opened up, which was basically a casino where anyone could play roulette, black jack and other card games. Most of us only rarely visited the place, but one particular airman became a regular visitor, and it was not long before he was thousands of pounds in debt.

The airman in question was only a leading aircraftsman, and when he realised that he could no longer service his debt to the casino he took drastic action. He disappeared overnight but left a note on his door stating that should anyone ever find his body then he wanted to be cremated. As it happened he had no intention of committing suicide, and a few weeks later he was picked up at Prestwick Airport while trying to board a flight to New York. It was a shame because he was a really nice person until he got caught by the dreaded gambling bug.

CHAPTER 16

Routine Orders

The NAAFI at Manston complex contained a billiards room that had a single full-size table, a television room with a single television and a large lounge bar. There were about a dozen chairs in the television room and whoever got there first chose what station to watch, but in those days there were only two television channels anyway, BBC and ITV (southern). The most popular programme was 'Tom & Jerry' and every time the credits came up with the name of Fred Quimby, it was normal for everyone to shout, 'Good old Fred!'

Being right next to the airmen's mess, the NAAFI bar was very convenient and it was customary to pop in there for a pint after lunch, especially after a hard morning shift. It was during one such occasion that I was drinking at the bar, sharing a joke with Charlie the manager, when a flying officer walked in dressed in a flying suite.

'Have you seen any cadets around here?' he asked.

'No,' I replied, 'but if they come in later, who shall I say is looking for them?'

'Flying Officer Insol', he replied. 'Send them down to the AEF straight away if you see them.' He disappeared out of the door but came back almost immediately. 'I don't suppose you'd like to go flying would you?' he said.

Although I had already drunk three pints of beer and was looking forward to a quiet afternoon in bed before my night shift, I could not refuse. I thanked him and replied straight away that I would be most interested.

'Good! Then come down to the flight in ten minutes', he replied, 'and ask for Fred ... Fred Insol'. I did not need a second invitation and I quickly scoffed my beer down, jumped off my bar stool, fastened my battledress tunic and tidied myself up. Charlie suggested that it was not a good idea to go flying after drinking so much beer. He was trying to be helpful, but I was not to be put off by such a small point and I made my way to the AEF hangar.

Within a short while, I was being strapped into the cockpit of a de Havilland Chipmunk, an aircraft that most people think was only ever used as a trainer. To some extent that is true, but it did serve in an operational role with 114 Squadron in Cyprus. The unit was based at Nicosia and from November 1958 until March 1959 it utilised the Chipmunk for security and communication duties. I can only imagine that the aircraft were shipped out to Cyprus because it would not have been much fun flying them there!

After I had put my flying helmet on and plugged in the connecting jack lead, I could hear my pilot going through his checklist before he called me on the intercom and asked if I was comfortable. I said that I was and ready to go and seconds later there was an eruption of noise and lots of vibration as the engine burst into life. As we taxied out my pilot began to chat on the intercom; he told me that his day job was as a pilot with BOAC and that he flew Boeing 707 cargo aircraft. He claimed that he did not get much opportunity to do any 'proper' flying, and he asked whether I had any objections to doing some aerobatics. Rather foolishly, I replied 'No'; it was a decision that I was to regret!

We took off on the grass runway that was designated as runway 24, situated immediately in front of the control tower and adjacent to the western taxiway. It was a bumpy ride as we built up airspeed, then we were airborne, and using his call-sign 'Alpha 51', Flying Officer Insol called local control and asked for permission to operate in Pegwell Bay at up to 3,000 feet. His request was granted, and as there were no other aircraft in the area we were cleared to do aerobatics.

Flying Officer Insol called me on the intercom and asked, 'Have you ever done loops or barrel rolls before?' My stomach was already feeling rather fragile, but I told him that I had not, and when he asked me if that was alright, I was too nervous to refuse. Within a few seconds I felt the nose of the Chipmunk going down and we dived towards the earth with him reading the airspeed aloud; when we reached about 80 knots he applied full throttle and pulled back on the control stick. Suddenly we were climbing steeply and before I realised it we were upside down, with me hanging from the straps and feeling very strange. We seemed to stop momentarily before dropping back to earth again.

'How about a slow barrel roll off the top next time?' my pilot asked. My senses had barely recovered and my stomach was still at 3,000 feet; we dived towards the sea again, building up speed. Then it was back into the climb, and on top of the loop he rolled the aircraft, not once, but at least twice, and my stomach nearly came back into my mouth. I knew that if anyone was sick on board a Chipmunk it was the policy of the Air Experience Flight to make that person clean up the mess himself! That prospect did not cheer me up at all, but I think Flying Officer Insol realised how I felt and he suddenly announced that we were going to chase a Hovercraft across the Channel.

Ahead of us I could see the large red and white SRN 4 hovercraft of Hoverlloyd that had just lifted off the pad and was slowly heading across Pegwell Bay towards Calais. Flying Officer Insol put the nose down and we chased after it; before it picked up speed, we flew overhead, so low that the spray from its large rubber skirt seemed to wash over our aircraft. We followed the hovercraft for several minutes, and then after a final fly past, we headed back to Manston.

As we approached the airfield, Flying Officer Insol asked me if I would like to take control – I did not need asking twice! 'You have control,' he suddenly announced and as I twiddled the stick, I realised the aircraft responded exactly to my demands. We checked the Manston QFE, and as we manoeuvred into position to land, he asked me if I would like to carry out the landing? He reminded me that it was a long 9,000-foot runway, and all I had to do was put the aircraft into a shallow decent and head towards the runway threshold, because he would control the power and flaps.

On final approach he called the tower to get final clearance to land. Pilots of large aircraft with retractable undercarriages normally called 'Three greens to land' on final approach just to confirm that the gear was down and locked and confirmed by three green lights. Rather typical of those pilots who flew Chipmunks, Flying Officer Insol called, 'Alpha 51 finals. Gear down and welded!' That was just to confirm that he had not forgotten the procedure, even though there was no need for it.

As we crossed the coast over Pegwell Bay, Flying Officer Insol guided me by telling me to bank left, push right rudder, stick left a bit, straighten up, nose up and suddenly we were crossing the threshold. We made a bumpy landing, but I am sure that my pilot knew what he was doing, and covering the controls to make up for my mishandling of them. As we taxied back into the dispersal I realised that I had got over feeling sick and I wanted to do it all over again! Unfortunately the Air Training Corps had finally arrived and cadets were swarming all over the place, eagerly awaiting their turn to fly.

Flying Officer Fred Insol was a regular on Number 1 Air Experience Flight, and he was one of its most popular pilots. Many years later and by pure chance, I met the man who had trained him to fly the Chipmunk, Squadron Leader 'Paddy' Brown. It was during a visit to the Spitfire and Hurricane Memorial Building, when the elderly gentleman behind the counter asked me if I had ever served at Manston. I told him that I had worked in air traffic control and that I had regularly flown with the AEF, Fred Insol being the pilot I best remembered. Paddy Brown smiled and he said he had known Fred very well and had taught him to fly at West Malling. We chatted for quite some time and our meeting was just one of many such occasions that proved to me that it is a very small world indeed!

For the most part, the Chipmunks of Number 1 AEF were part of our daily lives, and they could be seen and heard most weekends and afternoons in the summer. Being small and light they caused very little trouble in the way of noise pollution, although on one occasion they did upset a local establishment. One afternoon there was no civilian switchboard operator on duty at the twenty-line air traffic switchboard, and so I found myself manning it instead. When I picked up the call on one of the outside lines I was met with an angry voice, 'Do you realise that my tiger has just had a miscarriage?' The caller was furious and claimed that an aircraft from Manston had flown so low over the tiger's compound that it had subsequently miscarried a cub!

I was unsure how to deal with his complaint so I put the caller on hold, which triggered a barrage of abuse. Having decided to put him through to the ATCO (Approach Controller), I left the line open so that I could listen in, putting my hand over the mouthpiece to hide my breathing. It turned out that the caller was from the Port Lympe Zoo that was owned by the influential John Aspinall. Whether it was actually Mr Aspinall, who had friends and contacts in very high places, or one of his managers, I never found out for certain, but I believe it was the man himself.

As he was bound to be when dealing with any member of the public, the controller was polite and listened to the man who refused to calm down. While the ATCO was still trying to deal with the complaint, one of the controllers came in and said that the call would have to be transferred to the CO. Wing Commander Scott soon asked us to look through the log book for details of all the aircraft that had taken off since early morning, and especially those who might have been in the area of Port Lympe.

There were no obvious candidates for the offence as it had been a quiet afternoon with only the Chipmunks of 1 AEF doing some local flying.

However, a quick scan through the log and a few quick telephone calls revealed that a Chipmunk had taken off at lunchtime to fly to West Malling for a major overhaul. Kent radar civilian controller Bob Jeffreys confirmed that the aircraft had indeed flown close to or above Port Lympe, and the mystery was close to being solved.

Rather typically, we never discovered what the outcome was; considering Mr Aspinall's connections, the matter might have eventually been referred to the MoD. The tiger's miscarriage was one of the most unusual complaints that I ever dealt with at Manston, and I dealt with a good few in my time there!

Our long-standing residents, the Britannia and the CL 44, finally departed in September 1969 when they were bought by other airlines. While they were at Manston they had been well looked after and every month a team of engineers from Gatwick had turned up to run the engines. They also moved the aircraft backward or forwards very slightly to prevent soft spots developing on the tyres.

We were surprised to see that the pilot who came to pick up one of the aircraft was a very flamboyant character, who wore a garish red shirt and sported blue rinsed hair. Even more noticeable was the fact that he was considerably disabled with only had one arm and one eye. I do not know

The Goodyear Airship on a visit to Manston in 1991. Several Thanet district councilors were given an opportunity to fly in it around the local area.

the name of the pilot, but many years later I heard about a one-eyed one-armed pilot called Stuart Keith-Jopp, who had been a flying instructor and had later served in the air transport auxiliary service during the Second World War. Whether it was Mr Jopp I shall probably never know, but there cannot have been too many pilots with only one eye and one arm!

The CL 44, G-AWOV, was sold to a new company called Tradewinds, based at Gatwick, which was effectively Transglobe Airways arising from the ashes. Tradewinds operated four CL 44Ds and like G-AWOV (N229SW), all were aircraft that had previously belonged to one of America's biggest freight airlines, Seaboard World Airways.

The Britannia, G-ATGD, went to a company called African Safari Airways, based in Kenya. After leaving Manston it was flown to Luton for a much needed major overhaul. It finally left Luton for Mombasa at the end of the month, and it was destined to fly regular services between Zurich and Kenya. Without the presence of the two large airliners, the airfield looked empty; for the first time since I had arrived at Manston, the ASP had no aircraft parked on a semi-permanent basis. That situation would not last for long; within a short while, eight USAAF Phantoms were diverted from Bentwaters and took up short-term residence. The aircraft arrived from Germany, but they and their crews had flown all the way from Vietnam and the Phantoms were in a bad state of repair. They clearly showed the wear and tear of flying combat missions, probably over Vietnam. In most cases, the battles scars and damage caused by flak or ground fire were well hidden by paint and patches of metal, but when one got close up they were quite easy to spot. Observing those Phantoms on the ASP was the closest I ever got the war in the Far East.

In October I was given fresh hope that I would soon be posted overseas when I was ordered to have a Yellow Fever injection on the 18th. Because there were only certain medical establishments that held the vaccine, I had to travel to Shorncliffe Barracks near Folkestone. After several hours of hanging around I was examined and injected by an officer with the rank of captain, who warned me that my arm might go numb for a while. He was right about that, but he failed to warn me about possible swelling; within 24 hours my arm was very swollen indeed. Despite repeated requests about my posting overseas, I was given no more information, and that reinforced my feeling that I must be destined to remain at Manston until I was discharged.

During late 1969, a number of new faces were posted into Manston including Corporal John Pulford from Northern Ireland, and Sergeant Ray Baker, a controller who had just completed his training at Shawbury. Both were to play a large part in my life over the coming years, and in the case of John Pulford, far beyond that!

John was a big man from Evesham with a strong West Country accent. He could best be described as a loveable rogue, and was always willing to give those of us without cars a lift, as long as we bought him a gallon of petrol. John was also a source of travel warrants, because he and his family always travelled by car and so he never used the ones he was issued. Like several other married men he was quite willing to sell them to the single airmen who went home more often. John and Ron Sadler became the regular corporals on my shift and they were good fun to work with. John became a doorman in Ramsgate and got us into a few venues for free.

Sergeant Ray Baker soon got his 'crown up' to make him Flight Sergeant Baker, but it made little difference to him because he was a quiet unassuming man and a brilliant controller. Because Ray had not been sent on a radar course, his only duties were in local control, but it was soon recognised by most officers that his cool head and confident manner made him one of the best in the business. Despite his dedication to the job, Ray always had time for a joke and a drink. He always called me 'Young Joe', and when he wanted an extra cup of tea or coffee he addressed me in such a way that I could never refuse his request.

On one memorable occasion I woke Ray up in the middle of the night to tell him and the ATCO downstairs that the Invicta Airlines DC 4 was on finals to land. The aircraft was not due for another hour or so, and there had been no radio contact, but that was not unusual as in the early hours they often left airways at Dover and only called when they were on extended final approach. On my return from the toilets downstairs, I thought I saw its distinctive red and green navigation lights, glimmering in the sky on the approach to runway 29. Several minutes went by and I was a bit puzzled as to why Ray had not confirmed the landing time of the aircraft. He called me on the squawk box and asked me to go upstairs.

Pointing towards the sky, Ray asked me, 'Do you know anything at all about astronomy, young Joe?' I was puzzled by this question and replied that I could recognise the Plough and one or two other constellations, but I was not an expert! Then Ray asked me, 'Do you think you can distinguish the planet Mars from a DC 4? You should be able to because you've just been looking at it, and I'll tell you something else … it's a lot bigger and brighter than a bloody DC 4!'

The red and green tinted lights were still glowing away in the south-east, and it was clear now that they were not navigation lights. As I went back downstairs I felt a fool for making such an elementary mistake, and to make things worse the DC 4 called up approach just as the controllers had gone back to sleep. The next morning Ray had a good laugh about what had happened, but by then everyone on the watch had heard about it and took delight in teasing me. It took some time for me to live that one down!

Among the new officers that were posted in was a young pilot officer straight from training at Shawbury, who had only recently passed out of Cranwell. He was the perfect example of the new breed of officer and was arrogant enough to think that he was not only superior to the senior NCOs, but better at his job than they were. Subsequently they nicknamed him 'Pilot Officer Prune' after the legendary wartime RAF comic strip character. Just like Prune, he thought he knew it all, and regularly made a mess of things.

In November after I had completed my year of training I was allowed to sit the promotion examination to senior aircraftsman. I had to take some revision classes under the supervision of Warrant Officer Thorpe, and we spent several afternoons in the education centre going through my old notes and previous papers. To my surprise, I passed with quite a good mark, and I was immediately promoted to the rank of senior aircraftsman.

There was no pomp or ceremony and not even a 'congratulations' from the SATCO. I was just given a chit by Corporal Abbott to take to the stores where I was issued with a number of badges bearing the 'three propeller symbol' that represented the rank of SAC. I sowed them onto my two uniforms myself, although the first time I went home I got my mother to take them off and sew them on again properly. Apart from a slight increase in pay, the only difference was that I could officially work without supervision, but I had already done that on many occasions anyway. But now I was responsible for my own actions!

As I had done the first year, I volunteered to work the Christmas Day shift. On Boxing Day, John Scotney invited Chris Jhuboo and me over to his place to spend some time with him and his wife Marjorie. Chris did not have many friends, and with his family being in Ceylon it was nice for him to be back in a friendly, welcoming atmosphere. It was a relaxing day with lots of nice of food and good music, as John was very much into music, especially Johnny Cash and the Bee Gees. Chris and I went back to the block that night feeling very contented.

CHAPTER 17

Sport in the RAF

After Christmas I went on leave to Manchester for the New Year. On New Year's Day I went to St Helens with my old school friend Phil Hamer to watch our local rugby league team Swinton play. We had been good friends for many years and our mothers had first met in hospital when they were about to give birth to us in 1951. Having lost touch with each other for a while after leaving school, we had recently met up again in a local pub and together with another old school friend, Carl Lingard, we were good mates!

We drove to the game down the East Lancs Road in Phil's minivan that he used for his work as a joiner with a local building firm. At that time, Swinton, along with Wigan and St Helens, were among the top rugby league teams in the country, and there was a big crowd at Knowsley Road for the 3 p.m. kick off. Ken Gowers and Alan Buckley were among the Swinton players who also played for Great Britain, and they had a big influence over the game. However, at half-time the 'Saints' were winning 12 points to 7. Fortunately, Swinton had a better second half and the match was drawn at 18 points each. This was one of several rugby league matches that I went to at around this time and I could describe 1970 as being a very sporting year.

Sport was seen as being very important in the RAF; everyone was encouraged to take part and time off was given for most games and events. J. T. Larter and Air Vice-Marshal Larry Lamb were two fine examples. The former played rugby union for England and the latter was a top referee in the same game. Despite its size, RAF Manston boasted some very good sportsmen that played a wide range of games and won a number of trophies.

There was a squash court at Manston but it was a game played mainly by officers; although those in the ranks were not barred from playing, they were not actively encouraged. There were some enthusiasts, however, and Bill Newman from ASF was a regular player; his opponents were mainly senior NCOs and officers. Bill did not play the normal sports like football, but he revelled in certain fringe events and was a member of the Station Small Arms Club that competed at Bisley. He was an excellent shot and he helped to win several competitions for Manston. It seemed that everyone found their own sport and their own level.

We had a good football team at Manston, and although I was not one of the best players, I was selected to play quite regularly and enjoyed the game. On one occasion we drove up to RAF Headley Court in Surrey to play a team from the Joint Services Rehabilitation Centre. None of us were really sure what went on there and when we saw some of the opposition, we were confident that we would win. A number of their players looked quite old, and one or two of them showed obvious signs of injury, with bandages around their legs and heads. We were sure that they would prove to be no real opposition for us fit young things, but when we kicked off it was a different matter, and within a few minutes we were a goal down. Steve, our corporal and physical training instructor had no idea how to counter what were effectively a bunch of old and infirmed men. One of them in particular, who looked old enough to be issued with a bus pass, was running rings around us; in a desperate effort to make things more equal, Steve began to make changes and I was one of the first players to be taken off. By half-time we were two goals down and our heads were hung low as we were lectured by our irate corporal.

The second half began much the same as the first half had ended, with the same bald-headed old man running down the wing and generally causing chaos by getting the ball straight into the box. We did manage to score a goal, but within a short while Headley Court scored again, and the match ended with them winning by 4 goals to 1. It was embarrassing to say the least as the average age of Manston's team was about twenty, while the average age of Headley Court's players must have been nearly double that!

Before we travelled back to Manston in the minibus, we were invited to tea and light refreshments in the lounge, where we were briefed on the role of Headley Court and introduced to some of the staff. The player who had won the match for Headley Court almost single-handedly was there, although we never discovered his identity. Someone later claimed that he was a former professional footballer called Jesse Pye who had played for

Wolverhampton and England. That is quite unlikely because he was running a hotel in Blackpool at that time, but whoever he was, the middle-aged mystery footballer had run rings around a team of twenty-year-olds.

On the way back we stopped off at a pub called the Green Man, and apart our corporal, who was driving, we all had a lot to drink! Unfortunately things got a bit out of hand, and after an argument broke out about whose fault the defeat was, we were asked to leave the premises. Fortunately, the landlord did not know that we were in the RAF, otherwise it might have lead to more trouble.

CHAPTER 18

New Pay Scales

The Mediator Air Traffic Control System was introduced on 1 February to coincide with the opening of the new air traffic control centre at West Drayton. It replaced the operations centre at Uxbridge and the RAF unit based at Heathrow Airport that facilitated military movements in south-east England. The only changes as far as we were concerned were that direct line telephone numbers were issued for every RAF station and civil airport in the country, and that made it easier for us to contact them.

Up to that point, many stations could only be contacted via the switchboard at Uxbridge, and in an emergency that could take quite a long time. Every operations room and every department had a separate number that began with a '7', and it certainly made our lives a lot easier. It was one of the first major changes to Britain's air traffic control system, but in many ways Manston still languished in the past. While most RAF stations were fitted with the modern Type 1 Radar, our controllers still had to work with the old Type 787, and it would be many years before it was modernised.

There were, however, a number of other changes around this time. In April 1970, the RAF, the Royal Navy and the Army implemented the biggest ever change to their pay structures. We were to get a significant increase in pay, but at the same time have to pay for our food and accommodation, which had previously been provided for free. Each station was assessed as to what kind of standard of food and accommodation it provided, for instance single rooms, four- and twelve-man rooms. As we had single-room accommodation at Manston, we paid significantly more than those airmen on some other stations.

Also for the first time, single airmen could apply to live outside of their station in a house or flat of their choice. Of course, even with the increased pay, most airmen could not afford it on their own, and it was only possible if two or three of them polled their resources together. Permission had to be sought before an airman moved off the station, and certain conditions concerning his availability were imposed, but once he had approval he could move out and avoid the dreaded monthly inspections by the station commander.

Virtually everyone I knew decided to stay on in the accommodation at Manston, although everyone was sorely tempted to move out. The problem was that most of us did not have our own transport and we would have had to have used the very irregular East Kent bus service. It was handy living only a few hundred yards from where we worked, and the prospect of struggling in and out from either Margate or Ramsgate was too much.

Even after the increase, my pay only reached £7 a week, which was hardly enough to live on, but somehow we managed. When we were broke, Charlie in the NAAFI ran a book and we paid him what we owed at the end of the week. That is something that we would never have got down town; living on the station did have some advantages!

CHAPTER 19

Troublesome Times

In 1970, T 33s (Shooting Stars) of the Royal Canadian Air Force were regular visitors to Manston and one or two aircraft arrived every week. The Locheed T 33, powered by a single Allison J 33 turbojet, was a lengthened and modified version of the F 80 and the most widely used jet in the world. The T 33s normally arrived on a Thursday or Friday afternoon, from either Sollingen or Zweibrucken in Germany, and departed the following Monday morning.

On one occasion, there was a potentially disastrous incident involving a T 33, when the pilot declared an emergency shortly after he had taken off from Manston. The Canadian pilot sent out a 'pan' message to indicate that his aircraft was in danger, and that he was in need of assistance. The transmission made on the approach frequency showed he was declaring a state of 'urgency' rather than one of 'distress' as signified by a Mayday call. The problem was that his aircraft was rapidly venting fuel, posing the immediate threat of an explosion in mid-air.

Fortunately that did not happen, and fifteen minutes after taking off, the T 33 was back on the ground on the western taxiway, with the pilot demanding to speak to the officer in charge of the Aircraft Servicing Flight. Within minutes a team of fitters from the duty shift were out on the western taxiway inspecting the aircraft, and it did not take them long to find the cause of the problem.

Just before the T 33 had taken off it had been refuelled, and the airman responsible had not replaced the fuel filler cap properly. The fuel filler cap had worked loose in flight and the pressure had caused fuel to vent from the tanks. It could have been worse had the fuel sprayed on to the hot exhaust pipe.

It turned out that there were mitigating circumstances, and although the guilty party was only a leading aircraftsman, he had been allowed to carry out the task unsupervised. Because of the seriousness of what had happened he was put on a charge (RAF Form 252) and he was very lucky not to be Court Martialled. The offender was a nice enough character, but I sometimes I found him a bit cocky and arrogant, often showing off in his high-performance sports car. He also had his own group of friends who considered themselves to be above the rest of us. I think his mistake brought him down to earth, but he was very fortunate to get away with a severe reprimand and a heavy fine.

In the months after being posted to Manston, the SWO, Flight Sergeant Goddard, gave up trying to enforce his strict regime of discipline and Bull. He probably decided that it would be better for the efficient running of the station to have a more relaxed atmosphere. Discipline was generally very light, and apart from the occasional intervention by the SWO during monthly barrack block inspections, airmen were allowed to get on with things without too much interference from anyone. However, despite the relaxed atmosphere, there were those who brought trouble upon themselves. In 1970, within a relatively short space of time, two of Manston's small community of single airmen were sent to military detention centres.

Military prison is a serviceman's worst nightmare, and ever since I had passed through the gates of Swinderby during basic training, I had been haunted by the prospect of being sent to Colchester, the most famous of them all. I had read a book called 'The Hill', the story of a military prison in North Africa, and it sent shivers down my spine. With such a small community at Manston, it seemed strange that two airmen should default at the same time. Although they escaped the horrors of Colchester, they were sentenced to twenty-eight days detention at RAF Northolt, the RAF's modern detention centre.

One of the defaulters came from my own section in air traffic control and the other airman was my old friend John, who worked on the Aircraft Servicing Flight. He was the airman who I had accused of trying to molest me shortly after I had arrived at Manston. He was still trying to 'work his ticket'. Of the two cases, the one involving the airman from air traffic was the most serious, and among other things, he was charged with 'false attestation'. We all knew that Tony had been in the army before he had re-mustered to the RAF, and it was claimed that he had given the army false details when he had originally joined up.

Tony's case was also complicated by the fact that he had written to the Chinese Embassy asking for copies of Chairman Mao's 'Red Book' to be sent to him, along with some other communist literature. That was not acceptable to the authorities, and he was considered to be a security risk. But Tony's false attestation and interest in communist literature had only come to light because he was being investigated for another incident that had happened some months before.

It was alleged that he had picked up a girl from a pub in Margate, driven her back to the CTE fire dump at Manston, and then tried to rape her. Nothing was ever proved, but it was a serious accusation, and both the RAF and civil authorities treated the girl's claims seriously. As a result, he was investigated by the Special Investigations Branch of the Military Police, who together with the RAF Police, probed into every aspect of his personal and service life.

The Military Police, especially the SIB, have ways of making things stick, and they dug up Tony's background and examined his past activities and lifestyle. None of us knew exactly what he was charged with, and all we heard was that he had been sentenced to twenty-eight days' detention in Northolt before being dishonourably discharged from Her Majesty's Service. We never saw or heard of him again.

The reasons why John had been charged were a lot simpler; he had gone on a drunken rampage in Ramsgate and had caused a lot of criminal damage. The incident began after he had had a tooth extracted at the dentist, with the help of a cocaine aesthetic. Immediately afterwards, John went for a drink down at the Admiral Harvey pub opposite the harbour. Had he stuck to a couple of pints of beer, he might have been alright. However, rather typically, he drank himself into a stupor. When the barman told John that he would not serve him any more drink, he reacted very badly, throwing a bar stool at him, which missed its target but hit line of optics and bottles behind the bar.

John then calmly walked out of the pub and across the road by the harbour where he got a taxi to take him to Manston, but the police had already been called to the scene and they knew who he was and where the taxi was heading. Not content with causing trouble in town, when the taxi arrived at Manston and the driver asked him for the fare, John refused to pay and swore at the driver. As the argument raged, John put two fingers up to the driver and strolled over to the telephone box by the guard room, where he ripped off the receiver from its cable and urinated on the floor. The police arrived on the scene as he was leaving the phone box and John, who knew he was 'banged to rights', did not resist being arrested, but went along with a smile on his face.

Having been charged by the police with criminal damage and various other offences, John was then eventually charged by the RAF for related offences and 'bringing the service into disrepute'. The civil authorities agreed to drop their charges, and John could have been Court Martialled, but he accepted the CO's punishment, and was given twenty-eight days detention in Northolt. Despite what he had done, we all felt that John was not really a bad person, but just very sad and misguided. We all knew he had a lot of personal problems that had made him desperate to try and leave the RAF. Some saw his actions as just another attempt to 'work his ticket', and most of us recognised that, for whatever reason, he was turning the practice into an art!

A few weeks later, after he had returned to Manston, John nearly got into trouble again, but on that occasion it was only something of a light-hearted gesture. I was going flying with Number 1 Air Experience Flight and it turned out that my pilot was Squadron Leader White, the OC Flying. John helped to strap me into the Chipmunk and then he plugged the jack lead for the intercom into the socket. When I put the flying helmet on, the squadron leader did a check over the intercom, and it was obvious from his actions that he could not hear me and it was clearly not working.

John took the helmet off my head and put it on himself then began to fiddle about with the jack lead connection. As he fiddled with the lead he mumbled, 'Every time this bastard goes flying something happens! I reckon he's a ******* jinx!'

Then I heard a voice come through the headset in the helmet that was loud and clear, 'It's working now!' said Squadron Leader White, 'I'll see you in my office when I get back.' John looked quite bemused, but after closing the canopy he jumped down off the wing and stuck two fingers up in the air in typical defiance of authority. I had a pleasant hour's flying with Squadron Leader White and I never did find out if he disciplined John. If he did it was probably no more than the usual 'rollicking'. But everyone thought it would only be a matter of time before John was charged again, and then discharged on whatever grounds. He got away with a great deal that others would have been disciplined for, and became a legend at Manston in his own time.

CHAPTER 20

Surprise Visitors

One of the good things about being at Manston was that, despite what was written in the diary or on the Movement's Board, we never knew exactly what was going to happen next. A particular example took place one morning shift when fog severely restricted the number of aircraft movements, meaning that the only landings that could have been made were those under GCA Radar control. Sergeant Ray Baker was the controller that morning, as he often was. It was approaching mid-day and the fog had just started to lift when Ray got up out of his seat to stretch his legs, when suddenly he declared, 'Bloody hell young Joe! What do you see down there?'

Looking out of the window down on to the grass runway 06/24 that ran across the Ramsgate road, we could see a small single-engine aircraft that we immediately identified as a Piper Cherokee. We had received no calls on the R/T, and it seemed very strange that an aircraft could land without us being aware of it, but that is exactly what happened! I immediately pressed the button on the squawk box and told Movements what had happened, and within a few minutes the air traffic Land Rover had arrived at the aircraft.

Over the Pye radio set we were told that the pilot of the aircraft had been heading for Southend but had got lost; he had seen the airfield through a break in the fog and decided to try and land. The aircraft was taxied over to Invicta Air Cargo who reluctantly agreed to handle it. There were three men on board the aircraft who were all heading north to the races at Doncaster, and one of them was a well-known jockey.

Despite that, there were suspicious circumstances to suggest that the men had been attempting to enter the country illegally, and that they had only landed at Manston because of the bad weather. The pilot had not filed a flight plan and only held a basic private pilot's license with no Instrument Meteorological Conditions (IMC) that authorised him to fly at night or in cloud. Only after Customs had questioned the pilot and his passengers at length were they authorised to take off for Doncaster, and only then when the fog had finally cleared at lunch time.

One of the rarest visitors that I saw at Manston was a Cat Air Lockheed Constellation, an ex-Air France aircraft that carried the registration F-BHMI. The aircraft landed one afternoon carrying a number of race horses that were racing at a meeting somewhere in the south of England. It was parked overnight on the Invicta apron and it left the next day flying back to France with the same horses. The large sleek four-engine aircraft was an impressive site, and it attracted a large number of visitors during its short stay. It was the only Constellation that I ever saw flying.

On another occasion we received a flight plan for an Armstrong Whitworth Argosy that was due to arrive from Wildenrath and clear Customs before departing again for Benson. The Argosys of 114 and 115 Squadrons were regular visitors to Manston, so nobody was particularly bothered about it until the aircraft appeared on final approach to runway 29. Instead of the Argosy, we had another rare visitor in the form of a huge lumbering Blackburn Beverley. As it appeared out of the mist everyone went very quiet – until it landed, when the phones started buzzing and everyone became very excited.

There was always a certain amount of friendly ribaldry between air traffic and the Aircraft Servicing Flight who called us 'shinees' because they claimed that we sat on our backsides most of the time, shining the seats of our trousers. When we informed them that the Argosy was in fact a Beverley, a number of expletives were shouted down the telephone. Most of the abuse suggested that we were a bunch of useless ★★★★★★★★ and incapable of telling the difference between one aircraft and another.

That was not quite true, and there was no mistaking the Beverley; it had a very distinctive shape, with a fixed undercarriage and a huge double tail fin. It was powered by four Bristol Centaurus 2,850-h.p. engines, and could carry ninety-four troops or seventy-four fully equipped paratroopers, and over 12,000 lbs of vehicles.

The type had entered service with the RAF in March 1956 with 47 Squadron, and it saw service with five different squadrons over an eleven-year period. The last Beverleys to fly were those from 34 Squadron, but they had been withdrawn from squadron service in December 1967. Although I had seen some of them on the scrap heap at Shawbury, I never in my wildest dreams expected to see a Beverley flying in operational service!

The Beverley that landed at Manston was serial number XB259; it was an aircraft that had never actually entered operational service with the RAF, but it had been used by the Royal Aircraft Establishments at Farnborough. It had taken part in a series of trials and experiments concerning supply dropping and testing the brake parachutes that were later fitted to the Vulcan and Victor. However, as it became surplus to requirements and the end of its flying days approached, it had been purchased by Court Line (formerly Autair International), based at Luton. The Beverely was destined to become a static display to draw in the crowds.

Being quite a 'rare beast', lots of people were drawn to the central taxiway area to have a look, and most servicemen were aware that they would probably never see a Beverley flying again. The air traffic Land Rover, 'Rover 1', made several visits to the aircraft, but I was not among those lucky ones who were allowed on board. The aircraft only remained at Manston for a short time and within the hour it took off again for Farnborough. As I sat in the control tower and watched it trundle down the runway and take off, I realised that I was witnessing a historic moment in aviation and felt very privileged!

I also felt privileged to see the last Gloster Javelin to fly when it arrived at Manston without any warning and completed a number of overshoots on runway 29. XH897 was a Javelin FA7 that had served with a number of RAF squadrons before being handed over to the A & AEE and converted to an FA 9. The aircraft was involved in experimental work on Concorde and the Panavia Tornado, as well as a number of other projects. The Javelin made its final flight on 24 January 1975, and landed at Duxford where it became an exhibit in the Imperial War Museum's aircraft collection.

As well as the Constellation, Beverley and Javelin, many other unusual aircraft, both civil and military, regularly appeared at Manston. In many ways the airfield was often more like a museum than a Master Diversion Airfield, and it was always an interesting place to work.

CHAPTER 21

AOC's Parade

As every former airman knows, RAF stations are subject to annual inspections by the Air Officer Commanding (AOC) of their regional group. Manston was no exception, and in May 1970 it was visited by Air Vice-Marshal Clementi for his annual inspection. The highlight of any such event is the AOC's Parade, when airmen are formerly drilled and inspected to prove their station's efficiency.

Approximately two weeks before the annual inspection took place, practice parades were held; each section nominated a number of airmen to carry out the parade on the day. The parades were held on the ASP by the side of the control tower, and unless one was on duty there was no escape from several hours of marching up and down. Air Traffic probably contributed more airmen than any other section, and the Aircraft Servicing Flight got away lightly as usual.

For all of us who were taking part, the problem was getting our kit up to the standards expected for an AOC's inspection. A lot of airmen regularly wore their best blue uniforms to work; after a while they lost their colour and the 'Air Force Blue' became a drab dirty grey! Equally, many of us had lost or thrown our boots out and there was a mad scramble to get some issued from stores. New boots cause blisters and we had just a few weeks or so to get used to them before the big day. In the end it was decided that we would parade in our best shoes, which needed lots of polish to bring them up to inspection standards.

Towards the end of the last week there was a mad panic to get things organised and it was decided that we needed one more final practice parade. It was to be held at 9.30 a.m., just when I was coming off a long 15-hour night shift; I was certain that I would be exempt from taking part. However, Sergeant Collins, who had recently taken over from Sergeant Shelldrake, decided that there were to be no exceptions!

I complained to him bitterly and noticed that a number of other airmen, mainly married airmen who lived in quarters, were on their days off and would have been available but were not nominated. There was quite a bit of bitterness between single and married airman and occasions like the AOC's parade highlighted the difference in how we were treated. Married airmen often got away with growing their hair down past their collars and growing long sideburns, while single men who did the same were picked up by the SWO for looking scruffy.

It was one rule for them and another for us. 'Scalees' was often used as a term of derision to describe married airmen. It was a word that originated from the old pay scales before the reforms of 1970; married airmen were allocated Scale 'E' pay and allowances. The pay structure might have changed, but the bitterness that single airmen felt towards their married colleagues was the same as ever!

On the morning of the parade I was absolutely exhausted because it had been a long night and I'd had no sleep at all. To add to my misery, the shift that was taking over from us was late because the minibus that brought the married men in from Sandwich had got caught in heavy traffic. By the time we handed over to them and left the control tower it was 8.20 p.m.

When I arrived at the airmen's mess, Bill and Fred had stopped cooking breakfast and were already preparing food for lunch. I could have argued with them and demanded that I receive breakfast even if it had only been some toast, but I was too tired. By that time I had less than an hour to go back to my room, wash, shave, get changed into my best blue uniform and get back to the control tower.

Because it was raining it was decided to hold the parade in the large black hanger on the civil side that was normally used by Invicta; we were driven over there in a J2 from the MT section. We were formed up in two ranks ready to be inspected by the CO, Wing Commander Scott, and as he was passing down the line I began to feel a bit light headed. Suddenly everything began to spin around, and although I was aware what was happening, I was unable to prevent myself from falling backwards onto the cold concrete floor.

The next thing I knew, I was in the ambulance being driven over to the medical centre. By the time I arrived there, I was able to sit up and walk into the centre unassisted. The doctor, a local civilian GP examined me and quizzed me about my health and what I had eaten in the last 24 hours. When I told him that had not had anything at all since the previous evening he became quite alarmed and called in the sergeant medic. They went outside to confer and when they came back the sergeant said that he would have to report the fact that I had had not eaten breakfast, deciding that that was why I had fainted.

He told me what I already knew, that not to take breakfast before going on duty and for me to collapse as a result was technically a 'self-inflicted injury', for which I could be charged. When I pointed out that I had worked a 15-hour night shift and effectively been on duty for over 17 hours they showed some sympathy. Also I had not had time to eat breakfast and even if I had, the mess had finished serving by the time I came off duty! The sergeant said he understood all that, but he would still have put it in his report. Fortunately, I never heard any more about it, but I was bit fed up with being persecuted after being forced into an extra duty that I should not have had to perform.

A few days later it was the AOC's parade and inspection, and it all went off well and in brilliant sunshine. The AOC, Air Vice-Marshal Clementi, arrived from Northolt at about 9 a.m. in a twin-engined Pembroke. I was positioned on the front row of the parade line, next to Gerry, a corporal who had only recently been posted into air traffic, and next to him on his right was Denis Todd, who was sporting his General Service Medal. The AOC spoke to very few airmen, but Denis was among those he chose to have a very brief chat with.

Having suffered several CO's inspections over the course of a few weeks, and having bulled up our rooms and the accommodation block, we were disappointed that the AOC never even paid us a visit. Instead he spent some time in the officers' mess where he had lunch before inspecting the sergeant's mess. It was all very formal and in some ways we were relieved that he had not visited our accommodation block, for it may not have been up to the standard that he expected.

I was on duty in local control that afternoon when the AOC's aircraft departed for Northolt, but the departure did not go according to plan. As the Pembroke began its take-off run down the runway, everything seemed to be going alright, but just as the plane should have been getting airborne, it began to slow down. As the aircraft came to a halt at the threshold of runway 11, there were some unclear messages from the pilot over the R/T to local control. Using the binoculars I could clearly see that someone had got out of the aircraft and was seemingly walking around and inspecting it.

A few minutes later it all became clear; someone had failed to remove the Pito head cover and the pilot had no indication of what the aircraft's airspeed was as it trundled down the runway. The ground crew on ASF should have noticed it, but ultimately it was the responsibility of the pilot who should have picked it up during his external pre-flight walk about. It must have been a very embarrassing moment for the AOC, but not half as embarrassing as it must have been for the pilot when he got back to Northolt. In air traffic we all had a good laugh about it, but one could only imagine the red faces and bad language of the crew of the Pembroke!

CHAPTER 22

Summer Madness

When the SATCO called me into his office one afternoon, I wondered what I had done wrong to warrant his attention again? I thought it might be to do with the incident on the practice parade, but the SATCO appeared to be in quite a good mood and I was in for a surprise. He told me that there was a Midsummer Ball to be held in the officers' mess in a couple of weeks time, and as he was the president of the Messing Committee, he was responsible for organising the staffing. He asked if I would like to work as a steward for a rate of £5 for the night.

I had recently worked behind the bar in the NAAFI on a few occasions, and it seemed as though my reputation as a barman had got around. However, I was still taken aback by his offer, but as £5 was the going rate, which was a lot of money, I immediately answered that I would willing to do it. Before I left his office he asked me if I knew anyone else who might be interested and I said I would ask around. When I told Jim Reeves about it he said he was broke, and as there was likely to be free booze involved he was doubly keen. Corporal Brian Atkinson also volunteered, and having served for many years in the air force he was a veteran of such occasions.

We were told to wear black trousers and a black tie over a white shirt. A day or so before the event we were given white 'monkey' jackets to wear, and I must admit that we all looked very smart and very much like waiters at a posh London hotel. On the night itself I was assigned to the main bar area along with Brian; we served all the main drinks such as beer, lager, wine and spirits, but without any money changing hands. Glasses of beer and lager were only served in half pints, and everything was very civilised!

Jim was assigned to the champagne bar, and so all he had to do all night was be polite and top up glasses of bubbly for the officers and their wives and guests. We did not have much chance to talk until late in the evening when things had quietened down. Then Jim brought over a bottle of bubbly and we offered him a glass of whisky, but as the drink began to flow, things began to get out of hand.

When Fred, the cook from the airmen's mess, came in with a bowl of prawns, things took a turn for the worse as we began to gorge ourselves on them and various other bits of food that had been left lying around. We began mixing our drinks and putting whisky and vodka into our beer; then someone suggested that we drink mixed spirits out of a half-pint glass, and very soon everything disappeared into a foggy haze!

The next thing that I remember was waking up on the grass at the back of the officers' mess, feeling very groggy. Tom, the MoD policeman, had found me sitting up against a tree and he bent down and asked me if I was alright. I was clearly not alright, because I had been sick several times and my head was spinning like a top, so bad that I hardly knew where I was. With Tom's assistance, I managed to stagger back to the block and bed, where I lay on until I came to in the cold light of day.

All of a sudden the stark realisation hit me that I was working on the morning shift and I had to be on duty in the control tower by 8 a.m. I threw off my monkey jacket that was stained with food and drink from the night before, and struggled into my working blue uniform. Glancing at my watch I could see that it was almost 8 a.m., so I did not have time for breakfast, just a drink of water to rinse my mouth out and check my appearance in the mirror. I looked like death warmed up. I had not had time to shave and was scruffy, even by my standards, but I made my way up to the tower anyway so as not to be late and get into even more trouble.

When I arrived at the tower I thought it was strange that the main door was locked and I could not figure out why. Rather than ring the doorbell I went round to the Met Office where my friend Tim was on duty. I was shocked to discover that, with my bleary eyes, I had misread my watch; it was not 8 a.m. but 6 a.m., and most of those on duty in Air Traffic were still fast asleep. That was the final insult, but at least it did give me the time to go back to my room and sober up before I started my morning shift.

As I walked down the corridor I met Keith from the communications centre who was dressed only in his socks and underpants; he angrily pointed out that there was a great pool of sick on the floor right outside his room. He had walked into the sticky mess on his way to the toilet and he was less than amused at the prospect of having to clear it up. I told him that I was not responsible for it and pointed out that the trail continued further down the corridor.

Further investigation revealed that it ended outside Jim's room, and when we pushed his door open, we found him lying flat on his back with a toilet seat wrapped around his head and toilet paper scattered all over the room. There was little doubt that Jim was the culprit, but it would be several hours before he woke up to discover what damage he had done. I struggled through my shift that morning with a king-sized hangover.

We were off the Sunday and Monday, but on the Tuesday afternoon when I turned up for duty the SATCO appeared from his office and said he wanted to see me immediately. He angrily reminded me of the events at the ball on the Friday evening and said that my drunken behaviour had been appalling and totally unacceptable. The SATCO proceeded to give me one hell of a rollicking, and told me in no uncertain terms that I would not be getting paid for my night's work. No one else would be getting paid either, as he claimed that we had drunk more than our wages worth of beer, wine and whisky!

I left his office with my tail firmly between my legs; I knew that if the SATCO had not already agreed my assessments for the year, they would almost certainly be less than average. It seemed that any prospect I might have had of eventually reaching the rank of corporal had gone out the window for good. That fact did not really bother me, but I did think that the sooner I got posted out to some exotic overseas destination the better it would be for me, the SATCO and the air force combined.

CHAPTER 23

Working with Invicta

During the summer of 1970, there was a national docks strike and thousands of tons of freight and goods were transported by air, with Manston becoming a temporary base for several major airlines. The strike boosted Invicta's business enormously, but much of their work involved handling and unloading the wide variety of aircraft that were involved in the operation. These ranged from the Dakota, DC 7, Britannia, Boeing 707 and civilian versions of the Lockheed Hercules.

The strike began on 15 July and the following day, the Home Secretary, Reginald Maudling, declared a State of Emergency and ordered 36,000 troops – soldiers, sailors and airmen – to be put on standby to help move perishable goods from the docks to their destinations.

Alaskan Airways, Interior Airways and Southern Airways were just a few of the companies that operated out of Manston during the dock's strike, and it was later rumoured that the latter had CIA connections. Arco was a Bahamian-based airline that operated DC 7s, and its aircraft and crews were based at Manston for some time, flying cargo to destinations all over Europe. Laker Airways also flew into Manston on a regular basis, and the Boeing 707, G-AVZZ, became one of Manston's most regular visitors. The aircraft that had been registered VH-EBD was one of two Boeings operated by the company. Both had previously been owned by the Australian state airline Quantas, and had been sold off as it purchased larger and more modern types like the Boeing 747.

The increased activity at Manston did not go un-noticed by the media, and rumours about 'strike breaking' by the services in general and by the RAF in particular began to appear in the local and national newspapers.

As regards Manston, the rumours were totally unfounded, but the story did manage to attract a camera crew from Southern Television that appeared in the early hours of one morning. The van was parked up on the main road by Invicta operation's building, and it was not long before they got the story and the evidence that they were seeking.

When a camera crew spotted a ramp worker loader walking up the steps of a CL 44, dressed in an RAF tunic, the rumours of strike breaking seemed to have some foundation. The pictures that appeared on the local television news that night were quite blurred, but we clearly recognised the man in uniform. The culprit was a young airman who worked in the communications centre; I knew him rather well because he had been at Shawbury at the same time as me on an air traffic course.

The subject of airmen moonlighting was a sensitive one anyway, and we had all been warned previously that permission had to be granted from the CO before we did any kind of work. Not only did this particular airman not have permission, but he had never even applied for it; when the CO found out what had happened, the proverbial 'brown stuff' well and truly hit the fan! A complete ban was imposed on all airmen doing any kind of work outside their duties in the RAF.

As a rule, when we worked on the civil side we wore civilian clothes so as not to stand out from the other workers employed by Invicta. Most of the permanent employees knew that we were in the air force, but to most of the other temporary staff we were just another pair of hands. We found out later what had actually happened. After working a late shift in the communications centre the culprit had gone straight over to Invicta instead of getting changed. In the chilly early morning air, the airman had gone back to his car and put on his battle dress tunic, and so was virtually attired in full working blue uniform.

A lot of people were very angry and it took quite a while for the row to blow over; the guilty party found himself *persona non grata* in the mess and the NAAFI. He had lost other airmen a lot of money and was effectively ostracised by everyone, including Invicta who refused to employ him again anyway! Apart from the regular shifts we worked over at Invicta, none of the airmen at Manston were directly involved in strike breaking, and none of us were among those troops that we now know were assigned by the government to break the strike.

The strike ended on 30 July and the dock workers voted to return to work, but goods continued to be moved by air for some time. Manston and Invicta Air Cargo remained very busy, and the airline, with its limited facilities and staff, was stretched to the limit. As a result, on 5 August I had a lucky break when I was offered a trip to go flying in a DC 4 to Belgium.

I had reported to Invicta for an afternoon shift that would normally have meant just loading or unloading aircraft, but one of the supervisors, Allan, approached me soon after I arrived on the apron and asked if I had a few hours to spare. He explained that a DC 4 was about to depart for Antwerp but he and the two air loadmasters were unable to take the flight as they were either already committed to other flights or were resting. I was informed that technically at least, the flight required the presence of a loadmaster, and as nobody else was available Allan asked whether I would do the honours.

I accepted the offer immediately and within a few minutes I was in the operations room where I was introduced to my pilot, Captain John Gibson, and his co-pilot. I was asked to sign a 'blood chitty', and then I was taken out to the DC 4 that was loaded with 7 tons of Embassy cigarettes. My duties were quite clear: to ensure that the cargo did not move in flight, and if it did, then to prevent it from shifting the aircraft's centre of gravity. It was also my job to make sure that Captain Gibson got a cup of coffee at regular intervals during the short hop across the Channel.

There were just three seats on the DC 4 at the back of the aircraft on the starboard side, and the cargo of cigarettes was packed into large brown boxes stacked in front of me and covered in cargo netting. Almost as soon as the cabin door was slammed shut the engines were started and the whole aircraft began to shake and vibrate, so much so that I began to think that it was falling apart. I had flown in piston-engined aircraft like the Varsity before and I expected it to be noisy, but the DC 4 was something else; sitting in my seat at the back I was genuinely worried about its airworthiness.

There was little time for me to change my mind, and within a couple of minutes we were moving out along the northern taxiway towards the threshold of runway 11. At every turn there were squeaks and squeals from the undercarriage, and as we ran on to the runway, Captain Gibson did not stop to do the usual checks, but immediately applied full power; before I knew it we were rattling down the runway and then airborne and over Pegwell Bay. At about 1,500 feet we turned onto a south-easterly track across the Channel.

I had little or nothing to do; having reassured myself that the cargo was secure, I approached the front cabin and tentatively walked towards the cockpit. Captain Gibson waved me forward and as he greeted me his co-pilot began to tell me what he was doing, but without a headset it was almost impossible to hear what he was saying. Standing in between the two pilots I watched as a ship that acted as a light house flashed below, followed by a number of other vessels that were steaming up or down the English Channel. When we crossed the coast at Blankenberghe, Captain Gibson told me to return to my seat for the landing and within a few minutes we were rolling down the runway at Antwerp.

Only after the cargo had been unloaded did I discover that Captain Gibson had been instructed to pick up some more cargo at Maastricht, but he assured me that he would return to collect me later that afternoon, when he was due to pick up a return load. The handling agent, a chap called Andrei who spoke perfect English, took me to his office in the main terminal building and gave me a cup of coffee. He told me that it was only a short walk into town and that there were some good bars there. Having been directed which way to go I set out walking through a built-up industrial area on the outskirts of the massive docks complex. It was a lot further than I had been lead to believe, but I eventually found a bar called the Café dan Drakken, where I spent a very pleasant afternoon.

The bar was very busy and after I had been there for a while, I got talking to a number of older gentlemen who had fought in the war. As soon as they discovered I was in the RAF I was given free drinks and became the centre of attention. I told them that I was not a pilot but just an aircraftsman working in air traffic, but that made no difference to them. In broken English they told me of their appreciation for what the RAF had done during the war.

Some hours later I left the bar worst for wear, and made my way back to the airport where I had less than an hour before the Invicta DC 4 was due to leave for Manston. The aircraft landed just after I arrived back at the terminal building, but there was a slight delay because a large printing press had to be loaded on board. Eventually, I clambered up the improvised rickety steps and took my seat without making contact with the two pilots. Almost as soon as I sat down, the engines burst into life and within a couple of minutes the unmistakeable squeaky sound of the wheels could be heard as we taxied towards the runway threshold.

The runway at Antwerp was barely 5,000 feet long; just over half the length of the strip at Manston. Probably for that very reason, Captain Gibson sat at the end of the runway for several minutes before applying full power and releasing the brakes. The aircraft was shaking itself apart and the engines were screaming to be let loose, and then it suddenly leaped forward and began its take-off run. From my vantage point on the starboard side I could see the runway markers going by, and when we passed the half-way mark we were still on the ground with no sign of the aircraft getting airborne.

Just when it seemed that we were going to overshoot the end of the runway, the DC 4 struggled into the air and I breathed a sigh of relief. I do not remember much about the short flight back to Manston, and I slept for most of the time. I awoke just before we landed, and before I disembarked I went forward to say goodbye to the two pilots who were busy with their shut down checks. Having thanked the staff of Invicta Operations for the trip, I waddled off back across the airfield to my bed and I slept solidly until the next morning.

Things continued apace at Manston and large freighters like the CL 44 were regularly parked up on the ASP to unload their cargos of fresh fruit and vegetables. Lockheed Hercules of the RAF were also regular visitors, but we had not seen any civilian C 130s until Southern Airways began to fly in. Alaskan Airlines and Golden Nugget also operated C 130s and it was a bit of a novelty to see what was widely recognised as being a 'military aircraft' being used in civil role.

On 10 August I got my second flight in a DC 4 when I was asked to act as loadmaster on another flight to Antwerp with Captain John Gibson. By this time I was fairly familiar with the routine, and when we landed in Belgium the aircraft was unloaded and took off again to pick up another load at Maastricht. The only difference was that this time the aircraft did not return as it should have done and Andrei the servicing agent was sending Telex after Telex to Invicta Operations, desperately trying to find out what had happened to it. However, he was not as desperate as I was; I was worrying about how I was going to get back to England!

Eventually he established that the aircraft had gone U/S on the ground at Maastrich, but would soon arrive back at Antwerp approximately 3 hours later than planned. I had nothing to do, so Andrei produced a crate of lager beer, and we both just sat down talking and steadily getting more drunk. When we got the departure message from Maastricht to confirm that the DC 4 had taken off, we walked out of the terminal across the apron to meet the aircraft when it landed.

Captain Gibson apologised for what had happened and said that there had been a problem with one of the aircraft's engines, which had now been sorted out. There was a small amount of cargo to put on for the return flight back to Manston, and as soon as it had been loaded we taxied out and took off. The short flight was uneventful, that is until Captain Gibson was told that the runway at Manston was closed!

The main runway, 29, had been closed so that a foam carpet could be laid down for an aircraft that was having trouble with its hydraulics, which indicated that its wheels would not go down. The aircraft, which I think was a Canberra, had already made a safe landing on the foam carpet and after being closed down, it had been towed off the runway. The fire section was in the process of clearing up and washing the foam off the runway. Although the job was nearly complete, the controller said the runway was still closed until further notice.

We continued to orbit the airfield, and at about 3,000 feet, from my position standing behind the two pilots, the runway appeared to be clear; Captain Gibson decided that he was going to land anyway! I was ordered back to my seat and we flew out back across Pegwell Bay to make our approach, but the controller still declared the runway to be closed. Captain Gibson told the controller that there were problems with an engine and he might have to declare an emergency if we did not land soon.

I could see that we were approaching the ground, and the next thing I knew is that we were rumbling down the runway, but not the active runway, a piece of concrete adjacent to it known as the southern sterile. This use of the sterile was not permitted because it was not swept or maintained, but Captain Gibson made a perfect landing without damaging the aircraft. As I wobbled down the aircraft steps, I was met by Senior Customs Officer Jack Hobbs, who asked me if I had anything to declare? Clutching the crate of Belgian lager in my arms I said no, and being a gentleman, Jack just smiled as I hiccupped loudly and nearly fell down the aircraft steps.

The use of the sterile strip without permission did not go down well with air traffic control, and I heard later that a huge row had broken out between the SATCO and Hugh Kennard, Invicta's managing director, about the incident. Captain Gibson left Invicta shortly afterwards, but I do not think that had anything to do with what happened that day.

By this time, Invicta's facilities were being pushed to the limit, and when their one and only Air Start Unit (ASU) went U/S, it left them in an awkward position. The units were used to start the engines on modern turboprop aircraft like the CL 44, Britannia and Boeing 707, and without it, the aircraft had to start up using internal power that often drained the batteries. That would have meant that airlines would have gone elsewhere, and so Invicta's engineers came up with a solution. They made an informal unofficial agreement with the certain members of the Aircraft Servicing Flight that they could borrow its ASU.

Unfortunately the station's engineering officer was not party the agreement, and the view was that what he did not know he could not complain about. Everything went smoothly for several months until the early hours of one morning, when the inevitable happened; some of Invicta's ground crew managed to blow up the ASU! I was in the tower at the time, up in local control, and it was not obvious what had happened because the noise was more like a loud bang than an explosion. We saw a bright flash coming from the direction of a CL 44 on the ASP, but we did not know what had happened. Crash 1 was sent to investigate, and we soon heard.

Two inexperienced personnel working for Invicta were responsible for the incident. They had never used or connected an ASP unit before, but were allowed to be involved in the start up procedure for the CL 44. Fortunately, the aircraft was not damaged, but the pilots had to start the engines using the aircraft's own Auxiliary Power Unit (APU) that probably drained the batteries.

When the engineering officer found out what had happened to the APU, ruined by civilians who should never even have had access to it in the first place, the proverbial hit the fan again! The CO was informed of what had happened and an investigation was carried out, but we never heard whether it got as far as a Court of Inquiry. Changes were made in procedure, and from then on the Aircraft Servicing Flight became far less involved with Invicta's operations. The familiar sight of the ASF Land Rover sitting outside the Jolly Farmer with shady deals being made inside over a few pints became a thing of the past, for a short term at least.

CHAPTER 24

Winds of Change

There remained regular opportunities to fly at Manston whether in the Chipmunks of Number 1 AEF or other civil aircraft. On one occasion a civilian pilot who had flown a Miles Messenger into Manston came up the control tower and asked if could do some Ground Controlled Approaches (GCAs) using the Precision Approach Radar.

He seemed fascinated by what went on, but especially the skill of the controllers, and he asked a lot of questions about the RAF's air traffic procedures. Having got the ATCO's permission to fly around the circuit and make a few GCAs, the civilian pilot asked if someone would like to accompany him to show him around the local area and point out landmarks such as Reculver Towers and St Mildred's Bay. For some strange reason nobody else was interested in going with him, so I volunteered to go flying in what was basically a vintage aircraft.

The Miles Messenger had been designed in the early '40s as an Air Observation Platform for the RAF, although it was commonly used to transport VIPs. The aircraft first flew in September 1942, and the civilian four-seat version was a popular touring and racing aircraft in the 1940-50s. With its triple fin and large glass canopy that surrounded the cockpit, the aircraft was very distinctive, and from my point of view it felt like I was flying in a greenhouse. I spent a very pleasant hour flying in the Messenger, and we did a number of GCAs that were a new experience for both the pilot and me.

On another occasion the Instrument and Radio Flight (IRIS) asked if anyone wanted to go on a night flight over London Airport in the Varsity that was calibrating the radar at Heathrow. Rather remarkably, despite my recent misdemeanours, the SATCO put my name forward. Steve, a senior aircraftsman and my old friend who worked in the communications centre, also volunteered. We took off at about 10 p.m. because around midnight and early morning was the only time that the work could be carried out safely, without interference from other air traffic.

After take-off we were allowed to go into the cockpit behind the pilots, although the real work was being done by a number of operatives who were sitting in the main cabin behind complicated looking consoles. The only drawback was that we were flying at 11,000 feet and Steve and I were not given oxygen masks because there were not enough to go around. Despite that, it was a pleasant and fascinating experience watching the glowing pattern of Heathrow's lights, and its large green Pundit beacon flashing the letters 'LH', lighting up the sky.

All went well until the work was almost done and suddenly I heard a dull thud behind me; I turned around to see Steve had fallen backwards onto the floor. He had hit his head on the bulkhead as he went down and there was a worrying few minutes as one of the crew from the cabin rushed forward to administer First Aid and emergency oxygen. The pilot was immediately informed and as the operation was finished anyway, he quickly put the aircraft into an emergency descent.

By the time the Varsity was down to about 8,000 feet, Steve had regained consciousness, and the lack of oxygen at altitude was blamed for his condition, not as he later joked, the five pints of bitter he had drunk earlier that evening. The next day he was none the worse for his experience, except for a lump on his head and a hangover that should have been negated by the oxygen!

These were just some of pleasant experiences that I had at Manston, shared with a number of good friends. However, by now I had been on Pre-Warning Rosters (PWRs) for over a year, and I was still no closer to getting a posting overseas. In many ways I was quite happy at Manston, but having signed on for only five years, I knew that if I did not get abroad soon, I would probably remain at Manston for the rest of my service.

There were a lot of comings and goings about this time, and every time I read station routine orders and saw that some of those I knew were being posted to exotic faraway places, I began to get itchy feet. Fortunately, none of our little gang was among them, and the regular visits to the pubs in Ramsgate and Minster with Brian, Dave and Jim continued. Despite that, I could sense that things were not the same anymore, and I think we were all getting a bit bored!

By this time, the Buff Lodge was a popular place to drink and socialise, and it was very handy, being situated just across the road from our accommodation block. It had been set up and opened just a few months before by John Scotney, Denis Todd and Ron Sadler. Denis was the Grand Master and he had originally been part of the Ramsgate branch of the Royal Antediluvian Order of the Buffaloes that met at the Cannon Inn at St Lawrence. The order had its origins in Drury Lane where, in 1822, a group of stage hands had set it up as a sort of trade association. Like the Masons, there were a number of RAF branches.

The Buff Lodge was only normally open at weekends, and that was handy because that was when the NAAFI was closed, and the only other alternative if one wanted a drink was to walk across the airfield to the Jolly Farmer. The Lodge often had live music with groups and singers, and it was a very lively place on Saturday nights, but it was also open Sunday lunchtime, and that became a very popular session. Keith, who worked in the communications centre, was a regular on Sunday lunch, and he would wait for John Scotney to open up.

Keith would help John to clear up the tables and collect all the glasses left over from the night before, and then he would drink the 'slops'. The sight of Keith pouring stale lager, beer and other drinks into a single pint pot and drinking it down in one made us all feel a bit sick! He did it because he was always broke, and could rarely afford to go out drinking in the pubs down town; he said he hated to see good beer thrown away. He also drank from beer cans that had been left from the night before until he had a nasty experience when he discovered that someone had used one as an ash tray!

Sometimes during the week the Buff Lodge opened up and we drank there instead of going to the NAAFI. The actual building was one of the original huts that it been built as part of Number 3 Technical Training School, which had been based at Manston during the 1930s. Like many other parts of the station, it felt very creepy and there were rumours that it was haunted. John Scotney, a level-headed airman, thought it was all a load of bunkum until he had an unusual experience that helped change his mind.

On the night in question I saw John's car outside the lodge and decided that I would have a drink there instead of going into the NAAFI or trudging over to the Jolly Farmer. As I opened the outside door and pushed through into the lobby, I became aware that the place was in total darkness. I stepped forward cautiously and was making my way towards the bar area when all of a sudden the lights came on and I heard John's voice booming out from behind the bar.

'What the hell are you buggering about at?' I failed to see him to begin with, and I was quite surprised to hear his voice booming out. I was sure that he must be talking to someone else, but when he suddenly appeared from behind the bar it became clear that he was referring to me!

'What's the problem?' I asked.

'You are', said John. 'Creeping up to the bloody bar and messing about while I was trying to fix the lights.'

'It wasn't me,' I explained, 'I've just walked in here now.'

'So who was it who walked up to the bar, banged on the counter and then walked out of the door again?' John demanded. 'It must have been you!'

It took a bit of time before John began to believe me, and he explained that only a minute or so before I had entered the Lodge all the lights had suddenly gone out. As he had bent down behind the bar to check the fuse box he quite clearly heard someone approach the bar area, bang loudly on the bar as if they were waiting to be served, before walking back again towards the outer door. Outside it was a very quiet night and on the short walk from the accommodation block to the Lodge I had not seen anyone else around so there was no logical explanation.

The lodge certainly had a very spooky feel about it, and after that experience, John was reluctant to be there on his own. Several other people had similar experiences and claimed to have seen apparitions or to have felt as if someone or something had touched them. It was certainly not the place to hang about after a night out, and John and Denis often locked up and left together. Like the officers' mess, the sergeants' mess and several other parts of the camp, the old building had an aura all of its own, and it seemed to feel like it was in a different time zone. Whether it was just the result of an over active imagination I do not know, but it all seemed very real at the time!

In October 1970, things got a bit more interesting at Manston because of the arrival of Invicta Airway's first Vickers Vanguard, G-AXNT. Having had my first flight on the type in 1966, the Vanguard was my favourite aircraft, and the sound of its Rolls-Royce Tyne engines was music to my ears. Invicta used the aircraft on short-haul trips to European destinations like Ostend, and they very rarely carried cargo. Because of the modernisation of the fleet, we very rarely worked on the company's aircraft any more, although it continued to act as a handling agent for other airlines. There was still the occasional work for us as loaders, but the boom days of the docks strike had disappeared.

Invicta Vanguard G-AYFN on the apron at Manston with the control tower just visible in front of the nose. This former Trans-Canada Airlines (later Air Canada aircraft), previously registered CF-TKB, was leased by Invicta in April 1973 before being bought by the company. It was one of seven Vanguards operated by Invicta until 1976.

Other new types also began to be seen at Manston during late 1970. The sleek swing-wing F 111s of the USAAF began to use the airfield for training flights, making visual and radar approaches. The first two aircraft of a force of seventy-two F 111s arrived in the UK in the middle of September, and were assigned to the 20th Tactical Fighter Wing at Upper Heyford. There they joined a force of older types such as the F 100 Super Sabre, F 101 Voodoo and F 4 Phantom. The F 111s normally carried out high-level overshoots, often going around the circuit for an hour or more, before going back to Upper Heyford or Bentwaters.

Sometimes fighters from the USAAF would be accompanied by KC-135 air-to-air refuelling tankers (Boeing 707 conversions) that would overshoot the runway and then follow the aircraft it was working with along its route. To my knowledge, an F 111 never actually landed at Manston, but on at least two occasions F 100 Super Sabres were diverted to us. They were never very popular with the SATCO because on both occasions they caused a lot of damage to the runway threshold. While running up their engines immediately prior to take-off the blast from the tail pipes burned off the top surface of the tarmac and caused a large hole to appear.

After the first incident, the threshold had only just been repaired when a second visiting F 100 blew away the surface again, causing an even bigger hole to appear. It was true to say that our American allies were always welcome at Manston, although one way or another their presence often caused problems.

CHAPTER 25

The Red Arrows at Manston

The Red Arrows aerobatic team spent a lot of time at Manston during the early part of 1971 while the main runway at their base, RAF Kemble in Gloucestershire, was being re-surfaced. In 1970, Squadron Leader Ray Hannah, who had been the leader of the team for four years and probably the best known of all of them, was replaced by Squadron Leader Hazell.

SEE P. 194

The other members of the team that year were Flight Lieutenants E. R. Perraux, D. A. Smith, J. D. Rust, J. Haddock, I. C. H. Dick, R. B. Duckett, D. S. B. Marr, and R. E. W. Loverseed. It was nice having the Arrows around, and their presence enlivened the place, although the ground crews tended to be show offs, strolling around like peacocks in red overalls very similar to those worn by the pilots. That was especially the case in the airmen's mess, the NAAFI and the local pubs like the Jolly Farmer, which they effectively took over, along with the local women! It was against regulations to have women in our rooms in the accommodation block, but the Arrows blatantly paid no attention to that, and it was not uncommon to see females walking up and down the corridors and in and out of rooms. Even the SWO, who missed nothing, seemed to turn a blind eye, and we had to put up with being second-class citizens.

Manston was very busy during the first few months of 1971, and for a number of weeks the Red Arrows were short-term residents. Their Folland Gnats became a familiar sight over the airfield and above Ramsgate as they practised their various routines. Despite the skill and experience of the pilots in the team, between 1965 and 1971 the Red Arrows lost six aircraft and in 1969 they suffered their first fatality.

Seven Gnats of the Red Arrows flying over Manston in early 1971, when the aerobatic team was temporarily based there while the runway at Kemble was being resurfaced. For several months the Arrows were a regular sight over Manston and the Isle of Thanet.

On 26 March 1969, Flight Lieutenant Bowler was killed at Kemble on a training sortie when his Gnat, XR573, hit some trees while he was attempting to rejoin the main formation. On 16 December in the same year, another Gnat was lost after an erroneous call was made to inform the pilot that his aircraft was on fire. The pilot of XR995 ejected and landed safely while the aircraft crashed near Cirencester.

Towards the end of the year, things went from bad to worse. On 13 November another Gnat, XR994, was lost at Kemble after the pilot experienced an engine fire during a practice session. Just a few days later on 16 December, two more Gnats were lost and crashed near Cirencester, but like the previous incident, both pilots ejected and were safe. XR992 was abandoned after it was thought the pilot had experienced an engine fire, while XR995 was abandoned after its pilot mistook the frantic call over the R/T and thought that he was being told his aircraft was on fire.

It was inevitable that questions were raised in the House of Commons and the Red Arrows' future as the RAF's premier aerobatic team was in doubt.

Lord Carrington, the Secretary of State, gave permission for the team to continue for the 1970 display season, but with only seven aircraft and subject to the Court of Inquiry. It was not to perform the Roulette manoeuvre. Subsequently, when the Red Arrows arrived at Manston just a few weeks after the incident at Kemble, its future was very much in doubt, and every performance, training sortie and display came under close scrutiny.

During 1970, the Red Arrows lost only a single aircraft, when XR994 crashed at Kemble on 13 November after the pilot experienced an engine failure during aerobatics practice. The fact that the accident was caused by a technical failure and the pilot ejected safely prevented the incident from being added to the statistics, but in early 1971 the 'gremlins' returned with a vengeance.

On 20 January 1971, the team 'Synchro Pair' were practising the 'Russian Roulette', the most dangerous manoeuvre of all with a combined closing speed of 600 mph, when XR845, flown by Flight Lieutenant Haddock, and XR986, flown by Flight Lieutenant Perreaux, collided in mid-air. Both aircraft were totally destroyed. Flight Lieutenant Armstrong flying in the backseat of XR845 and Flight Lieutenant Lewis in XR986 were killed along with Flight Lieutenants Haddock and Perreaux.

One afternoon, early in February 1971, I was in the control tower when another incident occurred that could easily have ended up with the Red Arrows being disbanded. I was working in Movements when Mick Cocheran buzzed on the squawk box to tell me that nine Gnats of the Red Arrows were airborne for local flying. It was a quiet afternoon with just a few Chipmunks of Number 1 AEF airborne and a small number of civil and military movements. An Army Air Corps Scout flew in from Middle Wallop, and it was due outbound later in the afternoon to somewhere in Germany.

Approximately twenty minutes after the Red Arrows had taken off, Mick called down on the squawk box and said, 'Two Gnats down at ......' but then someone else, who I recognised as the controller, shouted in the background and overruled him with, 'No Red Arrows down ... still airborne ....'

The response was very confusing to say the least, so I called back upstairs and asked, 'Mick! Is that two Gnats or nine?' The controller answered the box again and said, 'Forget it ... it was a mistake .... Alright! All the Red Arrows are still airborne.'

It all seemed very strange and a few minutes later we were told that the Army Air Corps Scout had taken-off and was doing some local flying and a search over Minster. When I asked what kind of search I just got another abrupt reply from the controller that its crew were on exercise and I did not need to know any more about it! It seemed that the local controller had taken over the assistant's duties and Mick had seemingly disappeared. When the controller informed us that local control was temporarily out of bounds and we were not to go up there, I became very suspicious indeed.

A few minutes later, Mick came back on the scene and over the squawk box he shouted, 'Seven Gnats down at ......', but in the background I heard the local controller again, shouting even louder over him, 'Nine Gnats ... Red Arrows down at ......' Now I knew there was obviously something wrong. When the station commander came up the tower he went straight up to local control instead of going into the approach room, and I knew that something serious had happened.

All afternoon there were strange things going on with various members of the Red Arrows visiting the control tower, but also going straight up to local control without calling in to see us. We could hear the Scout helicopter hovering very low across the airfield, going backwards and forwards then disappearing in the direction of Acol and Minster. Eventually, Mick came down to collect a brew for himself and the controller and although he had an impish smile on his face, he was reluctant to say anything about what was happening!

When our watch finished at 5 p.m., Mick and I walked down to the mess together, but he still remained silent and would not give anything away concerning the events of the afternoon. Although we were the only two airmen in the mess, we sat and ate our meals in silence, which was only broken when Mick asked me if I fancied going for a drink later on. I took that to mean that he might be willing to divulge what had happened in exchange for a pint or three of Guinness, and so I readily accepted.

It was while we were walking across the airfield towards the Jolly Farmer that the events of the afternoon began to unfold, and Mick reluctantly told me what had happened. He said he was under strict instructions not to tell anybody, but he knew it would get out anyway, and so long as nobody outside Manston's service community got to hear of it then no harm would be done.

Mick said that shortly after the Red Arrows had taken off there had been an accident while the team was carrying out a manoeuvre called the 'Bomb Burst'. There had been a mix up and two of the aircraft had collided, with the wing of one Gnat hitting the nose of another, causing a substantial amount of damage to both aircraft. Fortunately, both pilots managed to maintain control of their aircraft and were able to make emergency landings without the need to declare an emergency.

The incident took the controller by surprise because it had all happened so quickly and the team manager who happened to be in the tower at the time had imposed an immediate ban on any details of the incident getting out. His decision was based on the RAF's 'need to know' policy. In the case of the Red Arrows, that included those of us who were working in air traffic control who were unaware of the events that had taken place.

The Army Air Corps helicopter pilot was actively involved in the cover up, and after being briefed, he spent the afternoon hovering around the local area of Minster and Acol trying to locate debris that had fallen from the aircraft. Some of the damaged components had fallen on the airfield while other pieces of the aircraft were eventually found some distance away.

To avoid arousing suspicion, the two damaged aircraft were pushed into the GEF hangar, out of sight of the general public, while the other seven Gnats were parked up on the central taxiway. Within a matter of hours, the Red Arrows had come up with a plan to obtain spares for the two Gnats and get them repaired without the authorities finding out about the collision.

A spare wing and a spare nose were procured from somewhere, and although we never found out where they came from, we suspected that Number 4 Service Flight Training School (SFTS) at RAF Valley in North Wales might have been the source. The reason being that when they were finally rolled out two days later, the Gnats in question had been fitted with a yellow nose and a yellow wing to replace the red damaged components. The only yellow Gnats were those that belonged to training units such as 4 SFTS, and it seemed quite likely that parts were requisitioned from contacts and friends without too many questions being asked.

Four days after the incident, we were on the morning shift when the Red Arrows departed for Kemble; in the half-light of dawn, the two damaged Gnats were the first to be pushed out of the GEF hangar. From our point of view, sitting in the control tower, the two Gnats with their temporary yellow surfaces clearly stood out. However, there were few people about to witness their departure, and within a few minutes they had started their engines and taxied up the western taxiway for runway 29. How things were dealt with when they arrived back at Kemble we never found out, but the fact that the accident had been kept a secret at Manston probably contributed to the Red Arrows continuing to be the RAF's premier aerobatic team for many more years.

CHAPTER 26

Final Adventures

On my last flight in a Chipmunk of Number 1 AEF there was some excitement to make us think that we had lost an aircraft. After a pleasant hour or so flying around the Isle of Thanet, we were returning to the circuit at Manston when we heard a Canadian T 33 working the approach controller. The Canadians always used the call sign 'Kiwi', followed by a number, so they were quite distinctive and easy to recognise over the radio. The T 33 was given priority to land and my pilot was told to clear the circuit to the south while the jet entered the circuit to land on runway 29.

We were about to switch frequencies to work the local controller on 124.9, when it became clear that there was a problem because we could hear the approach controller repeatedly calling the T 33 pilot but getting no response. There was no sign of the aircraft and so we continued to orbit Pegwell Bay, awaiting further instructions from Flight Sergeant Baker, the local controller. Over the background of the R/T carrier wave we could hear a tapping sound that was in a regular pattern, but we heard no voices other than that of the controller.

All of a sudden we saw a huge plume of black smoke rising into the air from a position somewhere to the north of the airfield, and my pilot and I both presumed that the worst had happened! It seemed too much of a coincidence that the controller should lose contact with the pilot of the T 33 at about the same time as black smoke began to rise into the air; we thought that it could only mean one thing.

For what seemed like several minutes, but what was probably no more than a few seconds, we were sure that the aircraft had crashed; as we approached the scene we expected to see the wreckage scattered on the ground below us. The local controller, Flight Sergeant Baker, was also convinced that the Canadian T 33 had crashed and had just reached out for the red crash phone to alert the fire section and medical centre when he had a call on the internal mini-com from the approach controller downstairs.

The approach controller told him that the T 33 was safe, but its pilot had lost the use of both his UHF and VHF radio, and was using the speechless code to communicate with air traffic. This information was received too late to prevent the emergency services from responding, and Crash 1 and Crash 6 had already left the fire section and were speeding down the western taxiway.

The approach controller who had been working the T 33 on radar had lost contact with the aircraft after it had disappeared into the 'clutter' that often appeared close to the centre of the radar screen. Having lost radio contact with the aircraft, he had naturally also presumed that the aircraft had crashed.

It was at about this time that we realised that the clicking noises we had heard over the R/T began had been the Canadian pilot transmitting on carrier wave, only on different frequencies for several minutes, but nobody had realised it.

Everyone was relieved that the aircraft had landed safely, and we soon found out that the thick black smoke we had seen had been caused by the Central Training Establishment (Fire School) having a 'burn up'. Someone on the CTE staff had authorised the aircraft dump to be ignited, but they had failed to notify air traffic control about the exercise. Later on, there were a number of harsh words exchanged between the SATCO and the Commandant of the CTE. He was told about what had happened and that in future air traffic control must be informed before CTE lit any fires for training exercises. Lessons had been learned all round!

Around the time of my last flight on a Chipmunk, I met an old friend from the past. Corporal Roger Darling, who I had last seen at Gaydon in September 1968, was posted to Manston. I had then just been a general trade assistant, and for whatever reasons, Roger and I had not got on well at all. However, when he arrived at Manston, things were very different and we laughed about the past, became friends and enjoyed some good nights out.

On one occasion, after a night out at the Jolly Farmer, we got involved in rounding up some pigs that had escaped while they were being transferred from a lorry onto an Invicta DC 4. The pigs had found the gaps in the fence and were running up and down the main road, enjoying their new-found freedom, but they were in imminent danger of getting run over by passing traffic. Fuelled by more than our fair share if beer, we ran after them and eventually got them back on to the Invicta dispersal.

After another pleasant evening at the Jolly Farmer, we very nearly got into trouble for attempting to board a Nimrod that had been diverted to Manston from St Mawgan. The first Nimrod had been delivered to the RAF on 2 October 1969 when it entered service with 236 Operational Conversion Unit at St Mawgan in Cornwall. On the night in question we were walking back across the airfield slightly the worse for wear when we heard the sound of the aircraft as it landed. We watched as it taxied down the western taxiway and parked up on the ASP. I am certain that this was the first time a Nimrod had ever landed at Manston, and we were all very excited and wanted to have a close up look at it.

As we approached the aircraft, the ASF Land Rover arrived on the ASP, and Bill Newman jumped out and began to marshal the Nimrod into position. After the engines were shut down, the steps were put alongside the cabin door and Bill and Rod went on board to ask the captain what his requirements were. Roger, Mick and I began to climb the steps towards the door when a large figure wearing the insignia of a master engineer blocked the way and challenged us.

'What the hell do you think you are doing?' his voice boomed. 'Get away from this aircraft or I'll have you all arrested.'

We tried to explain that we were in the RAF, worked in air traffic control and just wanted to have a look, but being dressed in civilian clothes, looking rather shabby and reeking of stale beer probably did not help to convince him. The master engineer told us that the aircraft was covered by the Official Secret's Act, and that if we did not go away he would have us all arrested, servicemen or not.

At that point a Land Rover drew up alongside the aircraft and an RAF policeman who had only recently been posted to Manston jumped out and walked towards the steps. He had probably been sent to provide the aircraft with a guard to protect it from the keen eyes of foreign powers, but as it turned out, the only threat that night was from drunken airmen! We were taking no chances though, and with our tails firmly between our legs, we quickly ran down the aircraft steps before scampering into the dark across the grass towards the control tower.

The Nimrod that was diverted to Manston that night was, I believe, an Mk 1, XV229; which had first flown in May 1969 and was extensively used for the development of the communications system. It was later converted to an Mk 2 in 1982, and when it was taken out of service after government cuts in 2010, the very same aircraft made the last flight of a Nimrod Mk 2. On 26 May 2011 it flew from Kinloss in Scotland to Manston where it was handed over to the Fire School. What an ignominious end for such a fine aircraft!

CHAPTER 27

Posted to Cyprus

We were on the morning shift on 28 January when Bill Williams rang up from the general office again to inform me that my posting to Cyprus had been confirmed and the date was effective from 1 May. He did not have a flight date, but he said that would follow, and I might not receive news of that until I went on embarkation leave.

It was great news, but the last few weeks before I was posted out from Manston were hectic and there were a lot of things to do. One job was to visit the stores and get measured up for khaki drill uniform. The stores section was actively involved in overseas postings, and it was also responsible for issuing a large wooden tea chest that would hold my most treasured possessions. It would travel to Cyprus ahead of me by sea, and so it would have to be dispatched several weeks before I left Manston.

Cyprus was a two-and-half-years' posting for single airmen, and three years for those that were married, and so there were lots of difficult decisions to make. Sorting through my worldly possessions I had to decide what I would take with me and what I would leave behind, but there was one thing I knew was destined to remain at Manston. Just before I received the news about my posting to Cyprus I had purchased a brand new state of the art record player from the Golden Wind music shop in Ramsgate.

The record player was too big and bulky to fit into my tea chest, and there was no other way I could take it with me. I reluctantly sold it for less than half of what I had paid for it. Despite the fact that the amount I got hardly covered the outstanding hire purchase payments, I had no choice and I threw in most of my records as well!

Other than having to sell my record player, I did have some regrets about the prospect of being posted out of Manston. I had a lot of good friends, and although initially I had hated the Isle of Thanet, I had grown to like the place, and I was particularly fond of many parts of Ramsgate and Broadstairs. I particularly enjoyed living by the sea and I often walked along the beach and cliffs from Ramsgate to Broadstairs. Probably because I had grown up in the industrial north-west, I had spent many happy hours just looking out across the sea, and I was fascinated at the movement of the many different types of vessels that ploughed up and down the English Channel.

When I heard that Brian was being posted to Germany and that Dave was probably going to be posted out soon as well, I felt better about things; if the old gang was being broken up, I did not want to stay at Manston on my own. There were lots of parties to organise and our nights out in Minster and Ramsgate became more frequent. One particular night out in Minster sticks in my mind. After drinking for most of a Saturday night in the Sadler and the Bell, we found another pub where we had a really good time!

The pub that was called the White Swan, situated at the bottom of the village close to the railway and the level crossing. It was near closing time at 11 p.m. when we ordered our first drinks, but rather surprisingly we discovered that the drinks were on the house! We thought that it must be some kind of celebration as there was free food being passed around and no one seemed bothered about the fact that it was well past closing time. Everyone was very friendly and although we did not know a single person present, everyone seemed to know us. We drank until the early hours of the morning and although the party was still in full swing, we reluctantly trudged up the road and across the airfield back to Manston.

The next day at lunchtime in the mess, all the talk was about the previous night's outing, and someone suggested that we go back to the pub to thank the landlord for giving us all a very good night. At the back of our minds we hoped that he might still be giving beer away as well! We got a lift down to Minster and were dropped off where we thought the pub should be, but in a matter of hours all the indications that the place had ever been a public house had been erased, and only the white paint and marks where signs had been removed gave clues to the building's former identity.

It was not until we got talking to a man who came out of a house a few doors down that we knew we had not imagined the events of the previous night and that there had been a public house on the site. He told us that the pub had only just closed down and what we had experienced had been the landlord's farewell party to get rid of the stock of beer. The building's

The control tower at RAF Manston on Wednesday 31 March 1999, the station's final day of service. The last of the service personnel can be seen flocking onto the balcony to watch the final flypast. During the 1960s and '70s, the tower was painted white, but sometime in the 1980s it was painted dark brown. It never looked the same again!

transformation into a private dwelling had come into immediate effect, and all indications that it had ever been a pubic house had been removed overnight.

We were very disappointed and I never heard anything more about the pub for many years, until it came up in conversation when I was relating the story of the 'disappearing pub' to a long standing resident of Minster. He told me that sometime after the new residents had moved in, some very strange things began to happen. Wispy white figures were often seen floating around the building and sash windows on the upper floor often seemed to open by themselves.

To the present day, strange things are said to happen in there, and no matter how many times the upstairs windows are closed, it is claimed that within a short time they opened again without any logical explanation.

My final weeks at Manston passed by very quickly and my official farewell party was held in the Buff Lodge on my last Saturday evening at Manston. It was well attended by both my friends and members of the Lodge. I had a very good night, at the end of which Sergeant Dave Collins from air traffic admin presented me with a pewter tankard. A raffle was held and one of the prizes (booby prize) was my pair of RAF-issue boots that, with the exception of a few parades, I had hardly worn since leaving basic training at Swinderby. I had forgotten to pack them into my tea chest anyway, which was by that time on board a ship and half way to Cyrpus.

My departure from Manston the following day was a very sad occasion, more so because I was still under the influence of the night before, and all I wanted to do was stay in bed and sleep. I ate my last meal in the mess alone, because everyone else was still sleeping off hangovers, and I suddenly felt that I was going to miss the many good friends that I was leaving behind. I failed to say goodbye to many of them, most of whom I thought I would never see again, but little did I know that within a short time I would be reunited with a few of them, while many of the others would remain good friends for many years come.

The two weeks' embarkation leave at home passed by very quickly, but by the time that I received the telegram with my movement orders, I was more than ready to leave again and begin a new life in the land of Aphrodite.

Aviation Terms and Abbreviations

A & AEE	Aeroplane & Armaments Experimental Establishment
AC	Aircraftsman Untrained (U/T)
ADF	Aerial Direction Finding
AEF	Air Experience Flight
AFM	Air Force Medal
AFU	Advanced Flying Unit
AOC	Air Officer Commanding
Apron	Hangar tarmac
ASCOT	Air Support Command Operational Training
ASF	Aircraft Servicing Flight
ASP	Aircraft Servicing Platform
ASU	Air Start Unit
ATA	Actual Time of Arrival
ATCC	Air Traffic Control Centre
ATCO	Approach Controller
ATD	Actual Time of Departure
BOAC	British Overseas Airways Corporation
CAATC	Central Air Traffic Control School
CIA	Central Intelligence Bureau
CO	Commanding Officer
CRASH 1	Call sign for Immediate Response Crash Vehicle
CTE	Central Training Establishment, also Fire School
DFC	Distinguished Flying Cross
EANS	Empire Air Navigation School
ECM	Electronic Counter Measures

ETA	Estimated Time of Arrival
ETD	Estimated Time of Departure
FLIPS	Flight Information Publications
GCA	Ground Controlled Approach
GCI	Ground Controlled Interception
GD	General Duties
GEF	General Engineering Flight
ICAO	International Civil Aviation Organisation
IFF	Identification Friend or Foe
ILS	Instrument Landing System
IMC	Instrument Meteorological Conditions
IRIS	Instrument and Radio Flight
LAC	Leading Aircraftman
LCN	Load Classification Number
MoD	Ministry of Defence
MT	Mechanical Transport
MU	Maintenance Unit
NAAFI	Navy, Army and Air Force Institute
NATO	North Atlantic Treaty Organisation
NBC	Nuclear Biological Chemical (Warfare)
NCO	Non Commissioned Officer
NOTAM	Notice for Airman
OC	Officer Commanding
OTU	Operational Training Unit
PAR	Precision Approach Radar
PBX	Station Telephone Exchange
QDM	'Q' code – a magnetic bearing
QFE	'Q' code – the aerodrome level pressure
QNH	'Q' code – the mean sea level pressure
QSY	'Q' code – change frequency
QTE	'Q' code – a true bearing
R/T	Radio Telegraphy
RAF	Royal Air Force
RED CROSS 1	Call sign for Medical Centre Ambulance
ROVER 1	Call sign for air traffic Land Rover
SAC	Senior Aircraftman
SATCO	Senior Air Traffic Controller
SFTS	Service Flight Training School
SHQ	Station Headquarters

SIB	Special Investigation Branch
SLR	Self Loading Rifle
Squawk box	A means of direct communication between one section and another
SUNRAY	Call sign used by station commander on Pye radio
SWO	Station Warrant Officer
TOG	Technical Problem on Ground
U/S	Unserviceable
UHF	Ultra High Frequency
VASI	Visual Approach Slope Indicators
VHF	Very High Frequency
VMC	Visual Meteorological Conditions
W/T	Wireless Telegraphy
WAAF	Women's Auxiliary Air Force